Napkin Notes

Napkin Notes

Make Lunch Meaningful, Life Will Follow

Garth Callaghan

with Cynthia DiTiberio

HarperOne
An Imprint of HarperCollins*Publishers*

HarperOne

NAPKIN NOTES: *Make Lunch Meaningful, Life Will Follow.* Copyright © 2014 by Garth Callaghan. All rights reserved. Printed in the United States of America. No part of this book may be used or reproduced in any manner whatsoever without written permission except in the case of brief quotations embodied in critical articles and reviews. For information address HarperCollins Publishers, 195 Broadway, New York, NY 10007.

HarperCollins books may be purchased for educational, business, or sales promotional use. For information please e-mail the Special Markets Department at SPSales@harpercollins.com.

HarperCollins website: http://www.harpercollins.com

HarperCollins®, ▆®, and HarperOne™ are trademarks of HarperCollins Publishers

FIRST EDITION

Designed by Terry McGrath

Library of Congress Cataloging-in-Publication Data
Callaghan, Garth.
Napkin notes : make lunch meaningful, life will follow / Garth Callaghan ; with Cynthia DiTiberio. — First edition.
    pages cm
ISBN 978-0-06-236344-2
1. Callaghan, Garth. 2. Cancer—Patients—Family relationships. 3. Fathers and daughters. 4. Conduct of life. I. Title.
RC265.6.C34A3 2014
362.196994—dc23

2014024721

14 15 16 17 18   RRD(C)   10 9 8 7 6 5 4 3 2 1

To Emma

826 napkins will never be enough

CONTENTS

Round Three

Round Four

When my daughter was an infant, I would often rock her to sleep in the glider we'd lovingly placed in her nursery just for this purpose. My wife, Lissa, spent many hours feeding Emma, so I thought it was the least I could do to take on the rocking responsibilities. To be honest, I treasured these minutes. The little sounds Emma made as she settled in to sleep. The way I could marvel at her tiny fingers, each miraculous eyelash on her eyes, the precious pucker to her lips. This was my time. To rock, reflect, relish.

Often our family dog, Lucy, would curl up on the rug next to us. She loved Emma and wanted to be in whatever room her "sister" was.

One time, when Emma was approaching her first birthday but

still allowed me to rock her to sleep, I looked over at Lucy. I don't know what made me think of it, but somehow I realized that one day I would have to explain to Emma that Lucy had died. Lucy was three years old at the time, and given the life span of dogs, I figured that by Emma's eighth birthday I would have to break her heart. I'd have to somehow find words to explain why Lucy wasn't with us anymore.

The thought brought me to tears. I didn't know how I could manage it. While I was all too happy to share with Emma the joys of the world, the thought of opening her eyes to the tragedies . . . No, thank you.

Little did I know that I would eventually have to sit down with her four times and tell her that I had cancer. To essentially lie to her four times as I tried to promise that I would survive it. I won't. I know now that this cancer will kill me. It is only a matter of time. Of course, I want there to be a lot of time, but recently my doctors told me that I have an 8 percent chance of surviving five years.

Emma is now fourteen. I have an 8 percent chance of seeing her graduate high school.

Those words are almost impossible to write. There are times when I can't face the reality of the end of my life. I'm not afraid of death. If I didn't have Emma, I would be able to say, "Well, it's been a good ride." I can't bear the thought of leaving my little girl, of not being there to watch her grow up, to provide counsel and advice, laughs and jokes. To be her dad.

So, I've had to find another way. I don't know how much time I have left. But I have discovered a way to every day let her know how loved she is, how much I support her, and how much I care about the person she becomes. I write her Napkin Notes, which I tuck inside her lunch bag every morning.

I share this book because none of us knows how much time we have left. Yes, we walk around the planet with the hope that we are invincible, but we all know life can be taken away in an instant. I have the "gift" of realizing that the end is coming. I can take the time to take stock and share with the people I love how much they mean to me. It's the only thing that matters. Your house, your bank account, your skills, your profession—none of it matters. It's all about the long-lasting relationships we build. That's it. That's the whole thing.

This book is a call. To wake up. Connect. Share your feelings. Make that phone call. Write that note. Because I know all too well the fragility of life and how important it is to take the time to connect with those we love while we're still here, while we still can.

Dear Emma, You can't steal second and still keep your foot on first base. Love, Dad

CHAPTER I

It All Started with a Napkin

I slowly folded the napkin and placed it in Emma's lunch bag. Lately my notes had turned to a baseball theme. Emma was developing into an avid softball player, and I loved using those analogies. I consider myself a base stealer, always looking for a new opportunity, ready to see what new directions life might take. But there was one instance when I dragged my feet. When I wasn't ready to run to second, even though that was what my team needed.

My wife, Lissa, is five years older than me. I've always felt so lucky that she chose me, a young whippersnapper, to be her partner for life. (Interestingly, my mom is five years older than my dad.) However, one of the challenges with being married to someone who is older is that sometimes I've had to jump into life changes before I was ready. I was the first of my friends to own a home. I married well before my best friends. Being a grown-up was thrust upon me over and over.

Early in 1999 Lissa came to me and stated frankly, "It's time." I am sure that there was more discussion leading up to this statement, but those two words were the ones that mattered. It was time to try to get pregnant. I was only twenty-nine, but Lissa was thirty-four, and it was time. We'd only been married for a couple of years, and I wasn't sure if I was ready for that next step. I had long prayed for a daughter, but I meant in the future. When I was ready to grow up.

I knew Lissa meant business. Honestly, I knew that the start of this adventure could be a lot of fun for me. Plus, it seems like everyone these days needs some type of fertility counseling, and I didn't think it likely that we'd get pregnant right away. I had time to get prepared.

Although we didn't get pregnant immediately, it didn't take long. The start of the adventure was over more quickly than I had hoped. I was facing fatherhood.

The next eight and a half months were a flurry of activity and preparation. We attended all sorts of classes. We chose a pediatrician. We spent countless hours in stores looking at onesies and other baby paraphernalia. We baby-proofed the house and prepped the nursery. (A hint to all the future dads out there: Build the crib inside the nursery! I loved building it so much that I got to build it twice!)

And of course, we read every baby name book published in North America. I strongly favored Elizabeth or Matthew. Actually, I wanted to choose Matthias, the German version of Matthew, but I knew I couldn't win that battle. I didn't even try. Lissa quickly vetoed Elizabeth due to a former roommate with whom she didn't get along. Lissa liked Benjamin and Chloe. Unfortunately, we had a cat, Ben, and naming our child Ben just seemed, well, weird. I vetoed Chloe because I envisioned playground taunts starting with "Chloe blowy."

After the twenty-week ultrasound, we found out my prayer had been answered. We were having a girl. My heart swelled as I was able to put a concrete image with the baby growing inside Lissa. A little girl. Finally, the reality of becoming a father was starting to seem more appealing.

And we were able to settle on a name. I had always liked the name Claire, for it carried with it an expectation of clarity. Lissa agreed. Claire Delany Callaghan was to be the name of our baby girl.

It wasn't an easy pregnancy. Lissa had morning sickness much of the first six months. She often lamented over our dinner choices as not mattering, since they wouldn't remain in her stomach long. Lissa's blood pressure kept rising, and there was a concern for her and the baby. I felt lost, not sure how to help, as many men do. It was my job to prepare the house for a new arrival, shuttle to various appointments, and stay out of everything else.

That Tuesday in October was an average day. I went to work as normal, and Lissa was headed to her doctor's office, to check her blood pressure. I received a frantic call from Lissa around noon. The doctor was concerned. Her blood pressure was creeping into a danger zone, and it was decided that we needed to have the baby. Today. I scrambled to pack up at work and rushed to the hospital. Lissa stood up awkwardly as she saw me approach in the waiting room. Her eyes were sparkling with anticipation. We both smiled. It was the day we would meet our Claire.

Once Lissa was admitted to the hospital, the waiting game

began. Lissa had been given oxytocin, and we were waiting for it to kick in. Lissa was hot, and I was shivering in the room. I curled up on the small sofa, fully clothed and covered myself with a blanket, to no avail. It was a long night. The oxytocin was working slowly. We watched the morning news and then game shows. I was anxious and felt pretty useless. I could get ice chips for Lissa, but other than that, I had nothing to do. Doctors and nurses came and went, each glancing at the charts and machines and seeing if things were progressing. After being in the hospital for twenty-four hours, it was finally time to push.

I wasn't ready.

Though Lissa probably recalls the pushing taking forever, all I knew was that suddenly the doctor was handing me an instrument and helping me squeeze the blood away from the umbilical cord so that I could cut it. I had no intention of cutting that cord! I had specifically told the doctor that I didn't want to! Yet here I was, in a room full of medical personnel, and I wasn't given an option. I gritted my teeth and did my duty, stepping back quickly as the doctor and nurses conducted the Apgar tests. Our baby, Claire, was here.

I wasn't ready.

I stood there, paralyzed. Not only did I not know what to do but I also didn't want to do anything. This was moving too quickly.

I wasn't ready.

Lissa quickly snapped me out of it. "Go to her!" she pleaded as she lay immobilized on the hospital bed.

I walked over to where the nurses were attending to Claire and I touched her gently. I still didn't know what to do, but I was present. I realized that this was it. It was happening. I was a father . . .

But I still fought that reality. After Claire was born, I went home to finally get some sleep. I hate to admit it, but the next morning I took my time getting back to the hospital. I had a nice quiet breakfast. Did the dishes. Took the dog on a walk. I didn't really want to go back to the hospital.

Eventually, I received a call from Lissa. "Um, honey, where are you?" I rushed back.

Our time in the hospital wasn't easy. Claire had a high bilirubin level and had to spend several hours of her first day of life in a small plastic box for phototherapy. There was our poor tiny hours-old baby, lying there with these goggles strapped to her face so the rays didn't damage her eyes. We couldn't hold or touch her during the treatment but could only stare at her through a window. It was torture. Yet somehow it made me start to claim her. That was my daughter in there, all by herself. Needing me. She started to seem like . . . mine.

What really helped me make the transition was when we finally admitted to ourselves that the more we were getting to know each other, and the more we hung out with Claire, the more we realized that her name somehow didn't fit. We had made a mistake. Our baby had the wrong name and it was our fault! We sheepishly asked a nurse what could be done. I imagined reams of paperwork and even going to court to correct this error. She smiled gently and told us this happened more often than we'd think, and there was a single form to fill out before we left the hospital.

We left that afternoon as a family, with Emma Claire Callaghan. I don't know what it was about the name. But once we changed her name, once she became Emma, she became mine. It became real.

As we packed her carefully into her car seat, and as Lissa eased gingerly into the backseat next to her, I took my place at the steering wheel, finally having an important job to do. I was taking my family home.

I looked in the rearview mirror. I couldn't see Emma in her car seat, but I knew she was there. My baby girl. And we were headed home.

I was ready.

***

Dear Emma, Sometimes when I need a miracle, I look into your eyes and realize I've already created one. Love, Dad

***

While at first my role as a father involved lots of diapers, rocking, and shushing, and focused on feeding, calming, and getting her to sleep, as Emma grew into a little girl my role changed. I soon realized that being a father was so much more than picking a name (something I'd already messed up) and keeping her fed. I was helping to form a little person. From first sounds to first steps to first words, my Emma started to have a personality. There was a little person in there. And it was my job to prepare her for the world.

It started with realizing that we really did have to teach her right from wrong, which meant discipline. I was never that good at it. She would just look up at me with her eyes full of hope, and no matter what she'd done, I'd want to cave.

Before I knew it, she was heading to school, and my hours with her each day were greatly diminished. We'd have time in the morning before school and work, some brief time at dinner and bedtime at night, and then whatever time we spent driving around during the day. I had only three times a day to directly impact my daughter: breakfast, dinner, and bedtime. When I added it up, it meant maybe one hour a day.

While I knew this was part of letting my child grow up and gain independence in the world, I missed those times of connecting. Of feeling like I shaped her day. I knew now that friends and school were taking up most of her waking hours, becoming more and more important. I wanted to find a way to insert myself into her busy days.

Emma has always been focused on meals. I don't know if other kids have this fixation. Emma would bound out of bed, blankie in hand, and ask, "What's for dinner?"

I was fortunate enough to work for a company that encouraged us to spend the time we needed with family. So, I became a kindergarten lunch volunteer. I opened milk cartons, squirted ketchup, passed out straws, and cleaned up spills. It was the toughest hour of the day. But it meant I was able to sit with my daughter for a little bit, meet her friends, and see how they interacted.

It also meant I was able to see what she was eating when she bought lunch from the cafeteria. I soon became an advocate for packing lunches from home.

I'm usually the first one up in my household anyway, so I became the expert lunch packer. I would chop, cut, mix, and pack. I'd try to throw in something special that I knew she'd enjoy, like a cookie or a pudding cup. Something to make her face light up.

Every now and then I'd include a note written on her napkin.

The notes started out very simple. *I love you. Have a great day. Be a friend to someone.*

I didn't even know if the notes were being read. I certainly didn't know if they mattered. But I wanted each day to be special.

One day, I had just finished making her lunch. I hadn't written the note yet. Emma saw the lunch bag on the counter without a note, and I saw the neurons firing in her brain. She scooped up the bag, came over to me with pleading wide eyes, and simply asked, "Napkin Note?"

That's when I knew it mattered.

So, this became a practice for me. A parenting practice. No matter what I had going on, I made sure Emma had a note. And as she grew up, the notes became more specific. More thoughtful. Sometimes I included quotes that were meaningful to me, like "Why fit in when you were born to stand out?" by Dr. Seuss. I realized that these were moments when I could help shepherd her, guide her into becoming a young woman. Being a father meant helping her become someone who would make a difference in the world. This was my little way of hoping to shape her every day.

I had no idea the napkins would one day become my legacy.

Learn how to take criticism with grace.

Criticism is an opportunity to improve. You don't have to jump into a defensive mode. First, thank the person offering a critique. Listen to the comment. Is there a way to turn the comment into something positive?

Remember when I commented on your batting? I mentioned that you should try keeping both hands on the bat longer. I thought you might be releasing the bat too soon and losing some power behind your swing. I saw resistance in your eyes. You ruffled at the criticism. I wasn't telling you that you were a bad person. I wasn't picking on you. I wasn't attacking you personally.

Criticism is not an insult. Accept it. It might be worth listening to.

Round One

May you live all the days of your life.

—Jonathan Swift

> If God sends you down a stony path,
> may he give you strong shoes. —Irish saying

CHAPTER 2

Sangria Red

I lost sight of her again. I was running, but she was faster. I had to stay on the path, but she was darting through the trees and the underbrush. I could not keep up. The path was too twisted and uneven. I was running up, down, left, and right on the dirt. The afternoon sun was beating down on me through the golden and red leaves. My wife and neighbors were well behind me, but we were all yelling her name. I was doing my best to run ahead, but I was already short of breath. I was scared. She hadn't been on her own like this, with so much freedom. I had to keep her within eyesight.

We were camping, an activity I didn't particularly enjoy. On a hike with our friends, our dog Noël had dashed off in pursuit of something and was nowhere to be seen. We had rescued her less than a year before. Noël had been in a local pet shelter for fifty-nine days. This nearby county shelter was not a "no kill" shelter, and after sixty days, the animals were euthanized. She was saved from that fate by FLAG (For the Love of Animals in Goochland), a local animal rescue group. Noël barely looked like a dog when we met her. She was just fur and bones. The fur she did have was patchy and sparse.

Noël had clearly been on her own for some time. She was skittish around most people and appeared to be deathly afraid of me. Lissa and Emma were certain: Noël was the dog we had to save.

I didn't want a new dog in our home. Lucy was my dog. I had chosen her and loved my German shepherd–Rottweiler mix for thirteen years. Lucy had died just four months before Lissa and Emma ambushed me with rescue dog pictures. I was still grieving and didn't want to have room in my heart for another pet.

I continued running even though my lungs felt like they might explode. Bailey, the neighbors' golden retriever, was keeping up with Noël, and I could just see a yellow ball of fur up ahead. All I could hope was that Noël wasn't that far in front of her.

Finally, I saw the dogs slow, some smell halting their joy run. I was able to catch up and put the leash back on Noël. I let out a huge sigh of relief, thankful that the rest of our weekend wouldn't be spent wandering the wilderness, hoping to somehow bring Noël home.

Our neighbors, Mike and Sheryl Bourdeau, had invited us camping, one last getaway before the cold of autumn set in. At least it was camping in a cabin and not in tents. I could handle staying in a cabin much easier than sleeping on the ground. We were celebrating Sheryl's birthday, and that night Mike had a fantastic dinner of steaks planned. We toasted the birthday girl with red wine and ate gourmet cupcakes. We played games and thoroughly enjoyed one another's company. The evening came to a close too quickly. As I was preparing for bed, I needed to use the bathroom. As I stood peeing, I watched in shock. My urine was sangria red.

I couldn't begin to think what was causing this. There was no pain. There was no other indication that something was wrong with me.

I commenced freaking out.

I found Lissa and told her what had happened. I grabbed my smartphone and tried to look up potential causes. There was hardly any signal. I stepped out onto the cabin porch, held my phone above my head, and tilted it at just the right angle to get a data signal. Blood in your urine was called "gross hematuria." I read through potential causes. At the end of a very scary list were two causes Lissa and I hoped could be the answer: vigorous exercise and an excessive amount of beets. Not only had I been running earlier, trying to catch Noël—an activity that isn't a normal part of my routine—but Sheryl's birthday treats had included a red velvet cupcake from a gourmet shop. Though I never would have guessed, Lissa suggested that the shop might have used concentrated beet juice to color the cupcake. We calmed ourselves down enough to sleep, hoping that it was a freak occurrence and not something to truly worry about.

The camping excursion ended without further incident, and I was almost unconcerned about what had happened. We headed home and resumed our normal lives, until I saw blood in my urine again the next day. Although I am not one to worry about little things, even I realized I should head to the doctor to have this checked out. I made an appointment with my general practitioner, Dr. Morgan.

After performing a routine physical, Dr. Morgan reported that everything had checked out okay, except for my urine. Dr. Morgan said, "This could be nothing. This could be something," but he wanted me to visit Virginia Urology to speak with a specialist. As I left his office, he told me that if I couldn't get an appointment quickly, I should call him so that he could expedite the schedule.

Fortunately, I was able to get an appointment the next day. I was paired with Dr. Tim Bradford by chance. We went through similar steps to those I'd taken with Dr. Morgan, and I noticed that Dr. Bradford used the same noncommittal phrase: "This could be nothing. This could be something." (Did they teach that phrase in medical school? To use when you really had no idea what you were dealing with? Was it supposed to put the patient at ease? If so, it wasn't working.) He ended with "Let's get a CT scan scheduled." He wanted to rule out anything serious. But he figured we might be dealing with kidney stones or something else minor.

Two days later, I was preparing for my very first CT scan. The process seemed regimented. Drink a disgusting white beverage called "contrast" at nine P.M. the night before the procedure. Drink it again ninety minutes before your scheduled scan. Don't wear metal. Drink some more contrast as you wait in the office. A serenity was imparted through this process. I didn't have time to be nervous or worried. I thought having a CT was above and beyond the diagnostic need.

The funniest part of the CT was the talk they gave me right before it started. I was lying prone on the metallic table, waiting to be inserted into the tube.

"Have you ever had a CT scan before?" the technician asked calmly. I shook my head. A slight smile stretched on the tech's face. "Okay. You'll run through the machine once. Just listen to the directions and breathe when you're told. The second time we'll turn on the IV contrast. Some patients feel a slight metallic taste in their mouths. Right after that, you'll feel as if you've wet yourself. Don't worry. It's not real." You know what? She was exactly right.

That little speech is part of the process. Set the expectations so the patient doesn't freak out when they feel like they've peed their pants. I hear the same spiel each and every time.

The CT didn't take long, and before I knew it, I was on my way home. Now it was time to wait. It would be five days before the results would be ready. Since I wasn't overly concerned with the results, I was able to focus on other things. My company had a weekend project for a local law firm. There was a Toys for Tots charity event I attended. I kept busy and waited to meet with the doctor.

> New beginnings are often disguised
> as painful endings. —Lao Tzu

It was finally time to meet with Dr. Bradford. My appointment was just before three, and Lissa needed to pick up Emma from school. I sat waiting in Dr. Bradford's office alone, my heel tapping the floor nervously. I figured everything was probably fine, but I still didn't like being there.

Just give me my clean bill of health or a recommendation to exercise more and I can be on my way.

It didn't go that way.

Dr. Bradford walked in. We looked at my CT on a computer screen, and the next forty-five minutes were a blur. I heard the words "tumor" and "twelve centimeters." I heard "biopsy" and "This is big enough, we'd have to get this out of you anyway." Then "The mortality rate is very high for kidney cancer that has spread."

My brain couldn't grasp what was being said. For crying out loud, I was supposed to have a kidney stone or something. Lissa wasn't even with me because this wasn't supposed to be something serious!

All I knew at the end was that Dr. Bradford was scheduling some additional scans to ascertain what exactly was going on in my body. I drove home in a fog. Though I knew he had said a lot of different things and discussed many various outcomes, all I had heard was "Mr. Callaghan, you are going to die."

As I drove, my hands gripping the wheel, I knew I was supposed to call Lissa. I'd promised I would check in as soon as I'd finished up. This wasn't something I could explain over the phone. I needed to share this news in person.

I drove faster, both dreading returning home and desperate to see Lissa. But as I pulled into the driveway, the garage was empty. Where was everyone? Didn't they know I needed them?

I am a patient person, but even I have my limits.

As I stood pacing in the kitchen, my phone rang. Lissa. They were on their way home. I shouldn't have answered my phone. I knew Lissa would ask questions, but I didn't know what else to do. She was my lifeline and I felt like I was drowning. I was frantic even for just the sound of her voice.

"How was the appointment?" she asked. I could almost see her in my mind, the road she was on, carefully driving our minivan, Emma in the backseat. The normalcy that enveloped her.

Everything was about to come crashing down around her.

Before I could avoid it, think of some way to stall until she got home, I blurted out, "I have cancer."

What was I thinking? What if she had an accident because she was distracted by this terrible news? But I wasn't rational. I was desperate. I was shocked. I needed someone to help me process everything.

They arrived home a few minutes later. Lissa ushered Emma into the kitchen to get a snack, then she met me in the bedroom upstairs and we hugged tightly. There were so many questions, and I didn't really have any answers.

Yes, the doctor was certain it was cancer.

Yes, I probably had to have surgery.

Yes, it had to come out of my body even if it was a benign tumor. It had enveloped my kidney.

Yes, it looked like it might have spread.

No, we don't know what caused this.

No, I don't know what to do.

Yes, I am in mortal danger.

Yes, I am scared.

No, I don't know how to tell Emma.

Learn basic car functions.

I didn't learn to drive until I was a senior in high school. Although my dad had taken me out in his truck on a backcountry road years earlier, I hadn't had much practice. I could drive well enough and follow the rules of the road, but I hadn't developed a high level of comfort with cars. They were pretty foreign to me.

One weekend I worked up the nerve to ask a girl to go to the Valley Brook Drive-In. Although Heidi said yes, she asked if she could bring a friend along. I thought that was weird, but I really wanted to spend some time with her and I agreed. I picked up the girls and we headed off.

This was an old-fashioned drive-in with speakers on poles and a playground for kiddos to play on before dark. We watched the movie and had a fun time. The trouble started when it was time to leave. I started my dad's truck, a Ford F-100 Stepside. I pressed on the gas, and we didn't move. What was happening? I didn't have enough experience to troubleshoot this, so I put the truck in reverse. Maybe I was hung up on something. We moved a bit, but not far or with any speed. I tried to rock the truck by switching between drive and reverse. I managed to spin up quite a bit of dirt. I also took out one of the speaker poles and a taillight. This was fantastic! What a way to impress a date!

I walked to the concession building and dropped a dime into the pay phone to call home. I told my dad what was happening.

He listened carefully and told me what to do. He said I should follow his instructions exactly. "Walk back to the truck, grab a flashlight, and pop the hood. Look around in the engine area for a couple of minutes and pretend you know what you're doing. Close the hood with confidence and get back into the truck. Start the engine *and take off the emergency brake.* Drive the girls home, and you can replace the taillight tomorrow."

Thanks, Dad.

Dear Emma, Anyone who thinks that sunshine is pure happiness has never danced in the rain. Love, Dad

CHAPTER 3

"I'm Excellent!"

I smiled as I put the cap back on my pen. This was a good one. When in doubt, my Napkin Notes tended to lean toward positivity or how you could change your attitude. This was a classic. I knew that the difficult times in life were often when you learned the most or were necessary to get you on the path to somewhere great. If you could keep that always in mind, you could get through anything.

I hadn't told Emma yet. I was trying to get her in the right frame of mind to hear my news.

When I was in college, I started working at a convenience store down the street. They needed a weekend clerk, and I needed a paycheck to help me pay for school. It wasn't an exciting or glamorous job. But it paid some bills. That was all I needed.

I had to get up before dawn on Saturday mornings for the first shift. Sometimes I even worked all night. It was exhausting, boring work. But I knew it meant I was helping with the costs of college.

One Saturday morning, when I had been working there less than six months, a man walked into the store. Stumbled was more like it. I couldn't tell how old he was, but he looked like he'd either just gotten in from a long night of partying or was just up with the worst hangover of his life. He wore a pair of glasses that I could tell weren't a normal part of his attire. He looked like the kind of guy who normally wore contact lenses.

He walked straight over to our coffee and started fixing a cup, slowing pouring in creamer and then stirring it with purpose. He looked up from his task and saw me. "How are you doing?" he said, probably not expecting a response.

I banged my fist on the counter and said, "I'm excellent!"

The man stopped stirring and looked up again, his eyes finally meeting my own. "That's an interesting attitude for this early in the morning," he said with a small smile.

"The more I say it, the more I'll believe it, so I'll get there eventually," I said honestly.

Before I knew what was happening, the man walked over to the counter, set down his coffee, and stuck out his hand. "Would you like a job?" he said.

It turned out the man worked at the Impulse division of Circuit City and he asked if I wanted to join their manager-in-training program. He liked my attitude. And it was enough for him to think *That's the kind of employee I'd like to have.*

If I didn't have that attitude, I wouldn't have gotten that job, which led me to meeting my wife, which led me to having Emma. If I didn't have that attitude, who knows where my life would be?

But having a good attitude about cancer? It was a test. Who wanted to have that word thrown at them at forty-two? Let alone to tell their twelve-year-old daughter.

A few days after my diagnosis, I knew it was time to tell Emma what was going on. I didn't know how much she knew about cancer or if I should even use that word. I wanted to spin this in a positive way and make sure that I had the right attitude about it, so I could keep her from being too scared. I kept reminding myself we really didn't know what we were dealing with yet.

Keep it vague and she'll never know how deeply this is scaring the shit out of me.

Lissa and I discussed for hours how to best have this conversation. Should we be together or should I do it on my own? Do we keep it from her? But I knew she could sense something was going on. I felt, in the end, that it would be better to explain to her as best we could, rather than have her feel left out and confused.

I couldn't help but think back to when I'd told her about Lucy. As I'd guessed when she was a baby, Lucy passed away when Emma was nine. While it was definitely a conversation I didn't look forward to, when I'd thought about it before, I hadn't taken into account how devastated I would be. I was just thinking about Emma. But when Lucy died . . . Wow. I was a basket case.

Lucy was the first dog I ever had. I never grew up with dogs, so when Lissa broached the idea of adopting a dog, I was reluctant. I didn't really know what this relationship would entail.

We visited several local pet rescue organizations without any success. I knew what I *didn't* want in a dog, but I wasn't quite sure what I wanted. And then one day we arrived at a shelter and I saw Lucy. I don't know how to describe it except that I knew the moment I saw her that she was the dog for me. She was a German shepherd-Rottweiler mix. An enthusiastic puppy. Every time we took her to the vet, he would look at her paws and say, "Oh, she's going to be a big dog—probably forty pounds." But each subsequent visit he would add another ten pounds. Lucy topped out at a hundred pounds.

After mellowing out following her puppy years, Lucy was the perfect dog. She was well behaved and never even needed a leash when I walked her. If I stopped, if she was ahead of me, she'd turn around and come sit by my side. She hated strangers and had a vicious bark, but if you crossed the threshold of our house, she was your best friend.

She was my dog. She always wanted to be next to me. I didn't realize how much a dog could give you. And more important, I never realized how much joy a dog expresses when you walk through the door, whether it's been five minutes or five days. Dogs certainly know how to make you feel important and loved.

And Lucy and Emma? They were truly sisters. Lucy was so patient with Emma as she grew up, got bigger, and wanted Lucy to be her playmate. There was one Christmas morning in particular when Emma received a toy hair-styling kit for Christmas. I walked into the living room with a cup of coffee to see my massive, hundred-pound dog patiently getting her fur blown dry and curled with the pretend tools.

When the summer of 2010 rolled around, and Lucy was thirteen, she started to slide downhill. She was sleeping more, eating less, having accidents in the house. We knew the time was coming.

That August I attended a Star Wars convention with my fifteen-year-old nephew in Florida. We were gone five days, and when I got home, Lissa approached me as I was unpacking my bags, still on a high from my experience. She sat down on the bed.

"I didn't want to ruin your time, but things aren't going well with Lucy."

I immediately stopped what I was doing, sat down on the bed next to Lissa, and listened to her talk about the vet visit. Lucy was dealing with liver failure.

"What did he say?" I asked. "Is there anything we can do?"

Lissa shook her head, her eyes filling with tears. "We could spend thousands of dollars on surgery but it would buy us a few months at most."

I sat there, looked at my hands. I hated that it had come to this. But I knew I just wanted to help Lucy. If she was so uncomfortable, we needed to do this now.

I went to the vet that afternoon and said good-bye to Lucy.

Emma was at a friend's house, and while I knew that it would be hard to explain that Lucy was just gone, I didn't want her to have to say good-bye. In so many ways, I thought that would make things even harder.

Then it was the moment I had been dreading for eight years. I had to sit down with my daughter and explain that Lucy wasn't here anymore. I had to break my daughter's heart, when mine already felt shattered into a million pieces.

It always seems impossible
until it's done. —Nelson Mandela

Emma was now twelve and truly growing into a young woman. She'd been exposed to the heartbreak of life more than I wanted. Just a few months before my diagnosis, my dad had unexpectedly passed away. He'd gone in for a biopsy to make sure he didn't have lung cancer, and a couple of days later his lung collapsed; he went into a coma and never woke up. Ironically, the biopsy came back clear. But it was too late. Dad was gone.

It hadn't been easy sharing the news with Emma. But her grandfather had been old. She'd had friends who didn't have living grandparents and she knew it was something that happened. But a parent being sick? Did she know the word "cancer"? I thought she would probably grasp more than I expected. I just needed to focus on the facts.

I sat down with Emma. I slowly broached my illness. I probably had cancer. I would have to have surgery. If everything went well, it would be cut out and that would be it.

I definitely minimized my fears. She cried. I held on to her tightly. I told her it would be all right, knowing that might not be the truth.

In the days that followed, I could hardly look at Emma, fearing for her potential loss. Yes, I was scared by the diagnosis and waiting to see what our treatment plan would be. But mainly I just kept thinking about Emma. About how young she was. About how difficult it would be for her to grow up without a father. About how much I would miss if I couldn't beat this.

I consider myself a fairly even-keeled person. It takes a lot for me to visibly show emotion. But I found myself standing in the shower, sobs racking my body. We were still waiting to learn exactly what we were dealing with. The diagnosis was vague, without a lot of positive options. All I kept thinking was that I could die within a year. I hadn't yet had a chance to make a difference in the world, with the exception of my family. Was that enough? I didn't know.

I tried to remember all the quotes I'd written to Emma over the years, looking through my list of favorite sayings. How could I dance in this rainstorm? How could I find a glimmer of light so as to see a rainbow, something I would never have seen if the rain wasn't there? But I couldn't find a glimmer of light. Anywhere.

Don't drink and drive. Ever.

I was young, probably around twenty. I was working in a nearby resort community and often had to drive home late at night. The road heading back to my small town was narrow—barely wide enough for two cars to pass each other without one set of tires going onto the dirt shoulder. It was a twisty and windy road.

One evening I stayed after work and went out with some coworkers. I probably had too much to drink. No, I definitely had too much to drink. I had no business being behind the wheel. I could have stayed with my coworkers. I could have called a parent. I could have slept in my car. I chose to drive home. I chose poorly.

I knew the road between Old Forge and Port Leyden wasn't easy to navigate on the best of days. I took a longer route that wouldn't be as difficult to navigate. I drove well out of my way knowing I couldn't stay on the road without having an accident. I was pulled over. Thank God. The officer clearly knew I shouldn't have been driving. I don't know why, but he didn't ticket me. He actually stood beside my car and talked to me for at least two hours. It was getting light out. I haven't the faintest idea what we discussed, but as the sun peeked over the mountains, he asked if I thought I could drive home safely at that point. I did, and he followed me to the county line. I made it home safely. More important, I made it home without injuring anyone else and learned a serious lesson that day.

I will always come get you. Let me. No questions asked.

> If you don't like something, change it.
> If you can't change it, change your attitude.
> —Maya Angelou

CHAPTER 4

Where's the Pony?

When I was in eighth grade Mrs. Nona Wiley (yes, I do remember *all* my teachers) shared a story with the class. The story went something like this:

There were twin boys. They were young—probably around six. Although the boys were twins, their personalities were incredibly different. One was extremely happy and the other was extremely anxious.

The parents took the boys to see a counselor. The counselor devised an exam. There were two rooms and the boys were separated. The anxious boy was taken to a room filled with every possible toy and

game. Imagine an Atari, G.I. JOEs, Star Wars action figures, a
PAC-MAN machine, a MERLIN, Stretch Armstrong, and more!
That boy sat in the middle of the room and cried. He was terrified
of breaking the toys and was paralyzed by his fear.

The happy boy was put into a practically empty room. There
were no games or toys. It only had a large pile of horse manure.
The stink was overpowering and practically unbearable.

The counselor was completely unprepared for the reaction of
the happy boy. He immediately ran into the room and started to
climb the pile of manure while simultaneously digging into it. He
leaped around the room and threw as much manure around
as he could.

The counselor looked on in amazement, finally asking, "What
are you doing?"

"With all this crap," the happy boy replied, "there has to be a
pony in here somewhere!"

I love that story. And I've always tried to be that second boy.

Everyone has hurdles. My dad battled alcoholism for years. I
grew up in a small town where many of the fathers spent hours
toiling as loggers or farmers. I have a relative who struggles with

depression. My mother and her sister haven't spoken in years. (You have to fix that, Mom. Maybe by the time this book comes out . . .) I have cancer.

I've long been a believer that it's not about the hurdle you face but how you try to overcome it. And overcoming hurdles can teach you more than a flat stretch of road. You learn to fight. To go into battle for what you want.

The first battle I remember facing was during tryouts for the Port Leyden Baseball Farm Team. Small towns have tryouts. Not everyone gets to play. It's simple logistics because there are only so many uniforms. Players have to survive the cut in order to get one of the coveted positions.

I walked across town, by myself, for the first day of tryouts. I had a new glove, and I was ready to play. Most of the boys in town were there, but the coach hadn't arrived. A few of the older guys were smoking. I thought that was weird. I didn't have any desire to smoke. Of course, they were all offering cigarettes to the younger kids. I refused, and one of the guys promptly threw a glove at my face. It hurt like hell, and I left, embarrassed. I shrugged my shoulders as I walked away. I knew I really wanted to play baseball. But the older guys clearly didn't want me there.

I didn't even make it back home before I turned around. The big kids weren't going to get the best of me. I marched back to the ball field and practiced anyway. I practiced every evening until the tryouts were complete. I loved baseball, and I was exactly where I was supposed to be.

I didn't make the team that year.

Although I would make the cut in subsequent years, I don't remember a single thing about those later tryouts. Why? Because there wasn't significant adversity. Those tryouts were unremarkable. I didn't have a battle to fight.

A champion is someone who gets up when he can't.
—Jack Dempsey

Cancer is the biggest hurdle I've ever faced. As soon as my doctor put the CT scans on the screen, even I, with no medical expertise, recognized there was something very wrong with my scans. I didn't completely understand the danger level, but "cancer" sent me into DEFCON I. I was presented with a battlefield on which I was a complete novice. How could I become a remarkable cancer patient?

How could I assist my doctors and help them to save me?

I had follow-up appointments scheduled for the first week in November. I knew I wanted to go in prepared, with as much knowledge as possible, so I could speak the doctor's language as well as possible.

Directly from the American Cancer Society website:
Although many kidney cancers are found fairly early, while they are still confined to the kidney, others are found at a more advanced stage. There are a few reasons for this:

- *These cancers can sometimes become quite large without causing any pain or other problems.*
- *Because the kidneys are deep inside the body, small kidney tumors cannot be seen or felt during a physical exam.*
- *There are no recommended screening tests for kidney cancer in people who are not at increased risk.*

I kept reading and learned:

- *About 1.6 million new cancer cases were detected in the United States in 2011.*

- *About 60,920 new cases of kidney cancer (37,120 in men and 23,800 in women) will occur.*
- *The average age of people when they are diagnosed is sixty-four.*
- *Kidney cancer is very uncommon in people younger than age forty-five, and it most often occurs in people fifty-five and older.*
- *The average growth rate for kidney cancer is less than one centimeter per year.*

I stared at the computer screen in front of me. How did this happen to me? I am only forty-two! Twenty-two years younger than the average age of diagnosis! And the tumor that they'd discovered in me? *Thirteen centimeters* at its largest point. Which meant that if it was growing at the average growth rate, I had had it growing inside me since I was twenty-nine. Essentially, ever since I had become a father, I had had a ticking time bomb inside me.

I continued to read. Kidney cancer is notoriously tough to defeat, and even when everyone thinks it's defeated, it tends to show up again years later. Kidney cancer doesn't really respond to chemo or radiation. How on earth was I supposed to win this battle?

I didn't want to feel discouraged. I knew—going into my next doctor appointment on Monday, when they would do a number of scans to figure out exactly what we were dealing with and our treatment plan—that I needed to feel like a warrior. I wanted to be the best and most aggressive patient known. No treatment would be off the table. I would jump into this crazy phase of my life and attack.

I am a self-described geek for many reasons. One of those reasons is that I am not afraid to admit how much I love Star Wars. I spent hours playing with Star Wars toys as a kid, and as an adult, I belonged to the Rebel Legion, a costuming group dedicated to doing charity work while dressed as Star Wars characters. Every time I thought about this battle I was facing, lines from my favorite movie would pop into my head: "Do what must be done." "Do . . . or do not. There is no try." "Luminous beings are we, not this crude matter."

I decided to wear only Star Wars T-shirts to each medical appointment, plus I would tell each member of my medical team why. I needed to differentiate myself. Be a person, not just a patient number. I knew how many countless appointments these people had each day. But Garth Callaghan? Oh yeah, he was the Star Wars guy. They would remember me. I would stand out. I would have brought a lightsaber to my appointments if I'd thought it would help.

The next few days flew by. I had a project in Rochester. A dear friend and colleague, Kim Zirkle, was managing the project. I told her what was going on and we commiserated together. The project was a success, but I truly didn't care. I couldn't wait to get home. What was I doing five hundred miles away from my family? This was crazy. I needed to get home.

I had a full set of scans on Monday: another CT, an MRI, and a full-body bone scan. Lissa and I went to the hospital for the day. I spent the day lying on various tables and staying still. Yet it was exhausting.

We went home. We had eight days to wait until we'd meet with Dr. Bradford and learn exactly what was going on. It seemed like an eternity. At least we had Thanksgiving to celebrate to take our minds off things. My mom arrived. We really tried to not let cancer overshadow the holiday. It was already difficult as the first holiday without my dad. Mom wanted to stay past her planned departure so as to be there when we got the results from my tests. But Lissa and I had our anniversary to celebrate right before the next appointment. I was bound and determined to celebrate as if it were my last opportunity. Maybe it was.

Finally, it was time to meet with Dr. Bradford. This time I made sure Lissa was with me. I needed a partner to listen and absorb what was being said. Dr. Bradford introduced himself to Lissa. We discussed the situation and then the scan results. My bone scan was clear. The cancer hadn't spread to my bones. The MRI indicated that the "spread" we had seen on the CT scan was probably not cancer but a cluster of blood vessels.

"So, this means . . . ," I said, trying to decipher exactly what the doctor was saying.

"It's good news," Dr. Bradford said. "While, yes, you have kidney cancer, it doesn't look like it has spread. So, we'll go in and try to take it out."

I looked at Lissa with a tentative smile. I was so excited to learn I *only* had kidney cancer. We would schedule surgery soon, and if all went well, I would resume a normal life shortly after the surgery.

As we gathered our things when the appointment wrapped up, I grabbed my bag and pulled out a gift for Dr. Bradford. It was a Star Wars medical droid action figure. He looked at it, puzzled.

I said, "This is the guy who saves the heroes. It's your job to save me."

Get lost in a country where you don't know the language.

It was my first day of school at Theodor-Heuss-Gymnasium in Göttingen. I was sixteen. I didn't know German. Sure, I could say a few things, but I was far from fluent. My host sister, Katrin, went to school with me and showed me around. She made sure I knew how to get back to the bus stop. I should have waited for her, but I was finished with my school day early. I was certain I could handle it.

I was wrong. I wandered the city and was completely lost. I hadn't the faintest idea where I was or how to get home. I didn't have a map. I was in a hopeless situation. I wandered the streets of Göttingen hoping to recognize something. I may have walked around for more than an hour. I ran into someone who looked familiar. It was the mom of my student liaison. She put me on the right bus home to my host family.

I was very lost. I didn't speak the language. I didn't have a cell phone. I lived. It's okay to be lost sometimes.

Dear Emma, It doesn't matter where you go in life but rather who is by your side and how you make a difference. Love, Dad

CHAPTER 5

My Gamer Girl

I was quickly learning how much this battle would be a waiting game. I just wanted to get into the hospital and cut the cancer out of me. Instead, we had to wait until right before Christmas. I hated that this was overshadowing what was normally such a joyous time of year.

My surgery was scheduled for December 20. Hopefully everything would go well and I would be back at home by the 22nd. It wouldn't be a normal Christmas, by any means, but at least, God willing, we would be together.

I purchased Christmas presents and helped to decorate the

house. I even flew out to Denver for a job interview. I had started the process of interviewing for this job before I was diagnosed. Once I learned I had cancer, it took on a whole new importance. I was currently running my own company and paying for my own health insurance, and I didn't have disability. I felt that if I could work for this company, I could protect my family. We didn't know what the future held, and I wanted to ensure the best outcome for everybody.

I made certain the hiring committee was aware of my health issues. A former colleague was a part of the interview panel and I pulled her aside, explaining what was going on.

"Well, I have surgery scheduled for December 20. There are three possible outcomes. One, I die on the table. Two, I have surgery and am fine and will be home in three days. Or, three, the surgery doesn't go well and I'm given a year to live, in which case I'm not coming to work for you." I was lucky to have a friend there who could explain all of this to the employer. They were supportive and understanding throughout the process.

One morning I paused as I watched Lissa washing dishes at the kitchen sink. I knew how heavily all of this was weighing on her. She was trying to be strong for everyone, keep the family running, and celebrate the holidays. I could tell her spirits were down. I walked over to her, hugged her tightly, and said, "I'm sorry. You didn't sign up for this." She replied, "Yes, I did. It was in the vows." She didn't even stop washing the dishes.

Facing this would have been so much harder if I didn't have Lissa by my side.

I sometimes like to joke that if we met today, we never would have gotten married. I'm a self-professed geek, and these days geek gamer girls aren't afraid to be who they are. But in the '90s, when I was looking for a wife, the only geek gamer girl I knew was my first girlfriend. Lissa has never even seen all the Star Wars movies. Sacrilege! Luckily, I didn't ask her that question until I'd already fallen for her.

Lissa and I initially had an on-again-off-again, long-distance relationship. We began dating the first time after meeting in Virginia at a retail managers' meeting for Circuit City. I lived in Syracuse, New York; Lissa lived in Richmond, Virginia. I was young, twenty-four, and Lissa was an "older woman" of twenty-nine. The difference in our ages really bothered me. We didn't date for long and didn't speak to each other for quite a while after I broke it off. We slowly became friends again but remained committed to a long-distance friendship. We even gave each other dating advice. Our long-distance phone bills were outrageous because we'd spend hours talking into the middle of the night.

One weekend my best friend, Ted McCall, came to visit. We were talking about this deep friendship Lissa and I had developed. I wasn't in a serious relationship, but I cared deeply for Lissa regardless of the distance between us. As we were discussing this paradox, Ted said, "You love her. It's obvious."

I turned to him, about to scoff. Then it hit me. He was absolutely correct! How did I not see that myself?

Somehow I found the words to express to Lissa that I wanted to give it another try. We started dating again, cautiously. We still lived five hundred and fifty miles from each other. And as a retail manager, I had to work most weekends. I struggled with committing to growing the relationship.

A few months later, I heard about a potential opening in the corporate office as a product manager. The position entailed being in charge of half the merchandising for my division, and it was a very coveted job. Not only was this a potential dream job for me but it would also bring me to the same city as Lissa! There would be no more three-hundred-dollar phone bills or waiting all day in an airport for a flight that never arrived! I would be able to actually see her, in person, more than once a month.

When I received the job offer, we rejoiced at the opportunity it would give our relationship. I moved to Richmond in late August, and I proposed to Lissa in October. We started to plan for a simple spring wedding. Although we certainly wanted to celebrate this event, we were frugal minded. We wanted to save for a house down payment rather than spend money on an extravagant wedding. If we had a simple wedding and a backyard cookout for family and close friends, we would still be just as married as if we had a reception that cost ten thousand dollars.

The simple wedding eluded us. We didn't have a backyard yet. Lissa's parents started to suggest banquet halls and send catering menus. Each day that passed seemed to increase the cost and our stress level.

A few weeks after our engagement, Lissa and I traveled to my parents' home for Thanksgiving. Thanksgiving with my family can only be described as an event that needs to be seen. My mother proudly declares Thanksgiving as "My day!" and steadfastly pounds her fist on her chest as if she were preparing for battle. We often have twenty-five relatives from around Northern New York visit for the day. Multiple generations squeeze around one another in the fifteen-by-fifteen-foot kitchen. The kitchen door is the main portal to the yard and is literally worn out from the children coming and going. Four of us sit around the kitchen table playing pinochle while dodging the shuffling of pots and pans. We even invite guests who are family only in spirit, although they are often smart enough to show up just shortly before dinner is served.

Mom was stirring or whipping something as Lissa and I complained about how our wedding plans and the potential costs were spiraling out of control. We shared the stress of menus and banquet halls. We weren't expecting advice or action. We received both.

Setting down the whisk and wiping her hands on her apron, my mom turned to us. "Why don't you get married here? Tomorrow."

I stared at my mom. Was she serious? We immediately came up with reasons it wouldn't be possible. "We didn't bring any nice clothes," I said, and Lissa added, "We don't even have wedding rings!" "And you have to have a wedding license at least twenty-four hours beforehand," I summed up.

We shook our heads. It was sweet of her to try to solve our problems, but it wouldn't work.

All of our protests were dismissed. Mom immediately picked

up the phone as she went back to stirring the gravy and called the town clerk. "Almeta, can my son and his fiancée get a marriage license today? Oh, you just finished dinner? Great. Steve can drive them right over."

And off we went. My dad drove us over to Almeta Szewczyk's house and we filled out the paperwork on her side porch, which was the town clerk's "office." We could be married the next day if we so chose.

If you want to go fast, go alone. If you want to go far, go together. —African proverb

---

We woke up Friday morning and set off for the closest mall, about forty-five miles away. We picked out wedding bands and asked for the "We're getting married today" discount. The salesperson almost didn't believe us, but we convinced him otherwise and also got the discount. As we then headed to a department store to find something to wear, I paused. "Do we really need to buy more clothes? Doesn't this defeat the purpose of an inexpensive wedding?" Lissa had already purchased a dress in Richmond. We looked at each other and realized that we'd be just as married if we wore the sweaters and jeans that filled our suitcases.

The drive back to my parents' house was the longest forty-five-mile drive I have ever experienced. I don't think we spoke more than a couple of words to each other. I know that my hands were glued to the steering wheel. I couldn't believe we were going to "elope" like this. It was so sudden. It was so unexpected and spontaneous.

While we were shopping, my family had been busy. They had contacted a justice of the peace, arranged for some flowers, set up chairs, and called my best friend, Ted, to come to be the best man. They even set up a Christmas tree for a nice backdrop.

We were married that afternoon. It was a simple ceremony. There were a few family members, a friend or two, and us. It wasn't our ideal wedding, but we're still just as married today as if we'd had something we had planned for months.

You may be wondering how my family could pull this together in the span of about eighteen hours. You see, my family not only had the spirit of helpfulness to make this happen but were also well suited to get this together. They were well connected to the town clerk, the florist, and the justice of the peace, and they had plenty of chairs for our few guests because my dad, Steve, was the funeral director in my hometown. We were married in the Cal-laghan Funeral Home.

There aren't many women who would be okay with getting married in a funeral home. But that's the kind of woman Lissa is and why she's been such a great companion and co-parent all these years. She's no-nonsense, let's get it done. And she approached this cancer battle with the same attitude. I was so glad she was still by my side.

When surgery day arrived, Lissa of course accompanied me. As I was wheeled out of the pre-op room, someone put heated blankets on me. What a wonderful, cozy, and safe feeling! I was more than ready for this surgery. I was ready for this battle to be over.

The surgery took longer than expected. The tumor had built a substantial network of blood vessels to feed it, and that network needed to be cut away. I woke up in the post-op room but was groggy. I was warm, and someone applied a cool washcloth to my forehead and neck. A nurse came by and asked if I had any pain. I apparently replied, as I pointed to Lissa, "Only a pain in my ass." Thank goodness I was still under the effect of the anesthesia!

But more important, I then realized I was still alive. Hopefully this nightmare would be over. I could go back to being a husband, father, son, brother, and employee. I was done being a patient.

LESSON #23:

Read the recommended reading.

I opted to take a European economics course while attending SUNY Oswego. I don't recall why. I wasn't particularly interested in economics and probably less interested in European economics. Nevertheless, there I was. The course had plenty of required reading, but the recommended reading list was twice as long. I struggled with the class and was earning a solid C by midterm. Most of my classmates were in a similar situation, but I felt I wasn't doing my best.

I decided to spend some time in the library and look at the recommended reading materials. There was a lot of content that applied to the class, and I started to understand more of the subject matter. I wasn't going to become an A European economics student, but I was absolutely going to earn something better than a C.

When the final exam was announced, the professor let us know the exam would be "open notes." I had spent hours in the library and taken pages worth of notes from the recommended reading materials list.

There will be many things you are required to do. Take a look at the things you ought to do too. They just might make things easier.

Normal is a setting on a washing machine.
Be awesome. —Unknown

CHAPTER 6

Messages with Meaning

I stood at the kitchen counter cutting carrots into sticks. My back ached, and I pulled over a kitchen stool to sit for a while. Dr. Bradford had said that many patients could return to an average desk job a couple of weeks after surgery. I don't know who the "many" patients were, but I could barely plod around my house in a bathrobe.

I tried to shake off the negative thoughts, but they stuck to me like cobwebs. I hadn't bounced back in the way I had expected, and I was tired and in pain most of the time. I felt like a failure.

The pain medicine caused me to fall asleep spontaneously, and

I would often wake up continuing a conversation I had started hours before. I stopped taking those meds about a week after surgery. I didn't need additional confusion in my life.

Lissa, Emma, and I tried to slowly move back to our "normal" lives. Christmas break was over. It was a new year. Emma went back to school. Lissa went back to work, this time full-time instead of part-time. Despite the "successful" surgery, we were scared. We knew the medical bills would start piling up and we wanted more income coming in. And although we didn't say it out loud, I think both Lissa and I were thinking that she needed a stable job in case . . . well, in case the unthinkable happened.

I definitely wasn't "normal" and yearned for normalcy. I didn't grasp this at the time, but my life would never be normal again. We'd constantly have to reset what normal was.

Despite the surgery being over, I was still scared of dying prematurely. (What is a premature death, anyway? Who's to say?) I couldn't sleep through the night. I woke up because of either pain or intense nightmares. I had never experienced violent nightmares before. Sometimes violence was forced upon me (bad guys breaking into our home or attacking my family); sometimes the violence was started by me (I would punch someone in the face or attack them mercilessly). These dreams were unnerving. I consider myself an even-tempered person.

I started a new job in mid-January as a national sales manager for Dish Network and flew out to Denver a month and a day after my surgery. I really wasn't ready to go back to work. It broke my heart to leave my wife and daughter for a week. Not only that but I was still recovering and in pain—physically, mentally, emotionally, and spiritually.

The week passed by quickly enough, and I flew home, grateful to see my family again. I expected to travel a bit for this job, but it would tear my heart out each time. Despite the fact that this cancer battle was over, it had scarred me deeply. I was clinging to my family, desperate to be with the ones I loved. I had learned that despite a successful surgery, I truly didn't know how much time I had left. Once you become acutely aware of your mortality, it's hard to put the blinders back on.

As each morning came, I was always the first one up. I'm an early riser, one to appreciate the dark of dawn and the quiet it provides. That was often why I was the one to pack Emma's lunch, and I always took a moment to write her a Napkin Note.

After my diagnosis, I would sit and stare at the blank napkins in the mornings. Even though I didn't want to admit it, I was afraid these notes might be the only things she had left of me one day. I started to see them as an opportunity to express the lessons that I would want her to have if I were to sit down and give her a "life's little instructions" book. Emma had just turned twelve; she was about to become a teenager. What kinds of challenges was she probably facing every day?

I knew how difficult peer pressure could be during this time. In fact, in the last few years I had started to say one phrase to her every time I said good-bye to her, whether it was in the house as I left for work or in the car when I was the one driving her to school that day. "Be yourself," I would say with a smile.

I didn't know why that particular phrase had become so important to me. I had never felt comfortable being myself growing up in the small town of Port Leyden. Port Leyden is a town of six hundred people, people who have lived a hard life. The people there use their hands to work. They are farmers, loggers. Athleticism and pragmatism are valued. I was the smart kid who liked sci-fi. I just didn't fit in.

When I was in sixth grade I had some teachers start to take me under their wing, encourage my academic endeavors. So much so that by the time I reached high school, I was excelling academically. I even had a guidance counselor, Mr. McSweeney, who put me up for a scholarship to spend a year studying abroad in Germany.

I didn't speak German. Neither of my parents had ever left the country. But somehow I knew, from the moment my teacher mentioned it, I was going to get this scholarship. I was going to live in Germany.

And I did. I spent one whole school year living with a host family in a suburb of Göttingen. I went from living in my small town of six hundred in Northern New York to a bustling metropolis where *everything* was literally foreign.

This was a turning point for me. When I went to Germany, I got to be myself. No one had a point of reference for me. And I thought all the German kids were different anyway. If they were weird, it was okay for me to be weird. I finally felt like I could be who I was.

I didn't want Emma to have to wait that long or to travel to a foreign country in order to feel comfortable in her own skin. So, in addition to my daily message of "Be yourself," my Napkin Notes took on that theme. I wanted her to trust herself. To not care what other people thought, especially when it came to superficial things.

"Look to yourself," I wrote. Then added, "You know the right path always. It's your choice to make the correct decision."

I looked at what I'd written with pride. That was exactly the kind of sentiment I wanted to express. To tell her that I trusted her. That she had everything she needed inside her.

I knew I was scheduled to travel for work the next day, so I took out another napkin. I often left a stack of napkins for Lissa to put into Emma's lunch box on the days when I was gone. I thought about how Emma might have been feeling about everything we'd been going through as a family. I chose a Japanese proverb that had always meant a lot to me:

"Fall down seven times. Get up eight."

LESSON #27:

Work as a waitress.

Waiters and waitresses work for tips. They can be the ultimate customer service providers, and they work on practically 100 percent
commission. Their job is pretty thankless. It's tough, physical work,
and if they're going to get paid, they need to be in a good mood,
friendly, courteous, a team player, and kind. These are great life
skills and will apply in any job.

I started waiting tables when I was twenty. I really wanted to
be a bartender over the summer, but I didn't have any experience.
You know what didn't require a lot of experience? Being a waiter.
It's grunt work. I was hired on the spot. I worked my butt off that
summer and learned a lot about both the food service industry and
life in general.

Being a waitress will make you a better team player. You'll learn
many of the basic job skills you need later in life. It will also make
you a better diner. You'll know both sides of the table. You'll never
under-tip.

> The value of emotions comes from sharing them, not just having them. —Simon Sinek

CHAPTER 7

The Napkin Note Notebook

After a few weeks, I had settled into a new work routine. One day I was working from home and was in the kitchen when Emma came home from school. She plopped her heavy backpack onto the floor and starting digging around in its contents. Her lunch bag came out, and I saw her go into the dining room, just a few steps away. Curious as to what she was doing, I peered through the doorway to see her pull out her Napkin Note and tear the napkin up.

I wasn't exactly sure what I was seeing, but I was shocked. *How bad was my note?* I thought, trying to remember what I'd written. Maybe she was just having a rough day.

I took a breath and walked over to her. I placed a hand on her shoulder and she peered up at me.

"Whatcha doing, honey? Did you not like the note?"

Emma's brows furrowed in confusion and then she realized what I was asking.

"Oh no, Dad, that's not it," she said with a smile. "Wait, I'll be right back," she said as she rushed up the stairs. A few seconds later (I was always amazed at her energy level these days since I still struggled to walk up those stairs), she bounded back down holding a black-and-white composition book. She handed it to me with pride.

I opened the book. Inside were my Napkin Notes, carefully glued in place and in order. She'd even written the date next to each note.

My eyes filled. I couldn't believe that she had taken the time to do this. And seeing the notes put together, with my handwriting and the personalized messages, made me realize how important these really were to her.

I bent down and gave Emma a big hug. "Thank you, Emma. This means so much that you . . . that you save these," I said, trying to keep my emotions in check. I sat on the floor and pulled her into my lap as we flipped through the pages. As I perused her collection, I saw through the pages and torn-off notes. I was looking at our connection, my expression of love and positivity, all neatly bound together. And that's when I noticed it. The date of the first napkin: January 6, 2012.

It was the day after she'd returned to school following my surgery.

My heart stopped. I knew that my illness had taken a toll on Emma, that she did her best to understand what was going on, but she was only twelve.

I gave her a squeeze. "What made you start saving these?" I asked gently.

She pulled away. "No reason. Just wanted to remember them." And she headed upstairs to find her mom.

Okay, maybe I was reading into it too much. She just wanted to start saving them. I didn't need to get all maudlin about it.

It wasn't until much later, when I'd started sharing the Napkin Notes and our story, that I learned my instincts had been right. A reporter from our local paper approached us about doing a story. Holly had somehow stumbled upon the Facebook page I'd created

Dear Emma, If I could give you one thing in life, I would give you the ability to see yourself through my eyes. Only then would you realize how special you are to me. Love, Dad and thought what I was doing warranted a lifestyle piece. Or at least her editor did. Emma and I did a phone interview together, on two different extensions of our landline. As we were telling the part of the story where Emma shared her notebook with me, Holly asked the question I had originally asked, which Emma had evaded. "Why did you decide to start saving the notes, Emma?"

"Well," Emma said, her poise remarkable, "we had just faced the first cancer diagnosis and his first surgery. I didn't really know what was going on, but I was really worried. I just knew that I wanted to have a piece of him with me."

In that moment, I was so glad Emma wasn't in the room with me. I was choking back tears. Heartbroken that she had sensed she might lose me. I had hoped I'd protected my daughter from my greatest fear. It turned out she was all too aware, and my Napkin Notes had been something for her to cling to, so as to keep me close, no matter what happened.

LESSON #29:

Learn to make a signature cocktail.

I bartended through my last two years of college. Not only did I build on my customer service skills but I learned to mix a pretty mean cocktail. Classics. Not the crap family restaurants blend together today and call their "signature" drink. Old-fashioneds, manhattans, martinis, whiskey sours, and sidecars—classic stand-bys. Yes, you should learn to pour beer and distinguish some wines, but mixing a cocktail is an art. It is always something that can be used in social situations.

Why is this important? Mixing a cocktail is more than combining some alcohol and a mixer. It's the start of a conversation. Your hands and mind will be busy, but you can take the time to listen. You are giving your friend the opportunity to sit back and talk to you. You might need to cut up some fruit or get some ice. This all takes some time, during which you and your friend can unwind and enjoy each other's company.

Garth's Signature Vodka Gimlet

1. Dissolve one cup of sugar in one cup of water.
2. Add an equal amount of lime juice to the simple syrup you just created.
3. Stir together vodka and ice in a mixing glass.
4. Add the simple lime syrup to taste. It should tint the drink slightly.
5. Pour, straining out the remains of the ice, and enjoy!

Five important things to remember:

Use quality ingredients.

Take your time.

Do your best.

Listen.

Talk.

Round Two

Yesterday's home runs don't win today's games.

—Babe Ruth

> *Learn as if you were to live forever.*
> —Mahatma Gandhi

CHAPTER 8

The Prostate Is Like Popcorn

It wasn't until I had Emma that I was able to truly understand my mom. My mom has always been what you might call a smotherer. You know the mom, Marie, from *Everybody Loves Raymond*? That is my mom. To a tee.

I'm the firstborn son, and I received most of my mom's smothering. Thus I have always held my mom at bay. I didn't tell her every little detail because she'd always want more. When I told her about the scholarship opportunity to spend a year in Germany, she burst into tears just because I had the possibility of leaving. Now that I have Emma, I can understand her reaction. Would I want my sixteen-year-old daughter spending a year on her own halfway across the world? Hell no!

But parenting is about letting go and focusing on what will best shape your child. Traveling abroad is a crash course in growing up. Realizing the importance of pushing yourself. Getting out of your comfort zone and how it helps you really grow and change. That year in Germany forever changed me. It not only allowed me to finally feel comfortable in my own skin but also opened my eyes to the fact that there are always two sides to everything. Germany was so vastly different from the United States, and while I had culture shock when I first moved over there, I also had culture shock when I moved back home. The cars were large; the people were loud. That experience made me diplomatic. I'm always able now to help people see the other side of things.

My parents could have said no despite the fact I had received a full scholarship. They didn't. It was out of their comfort zone, but they trusted me. They didn't want to hold me back. They knew it was something I needed. It instilled a self-confidence that I carry with me to this day.

I knew it was hard for my mom to support me during this cancer fight. She was still grieving her husband. And now her son was battling cancer? "The Callaghans are having a really bad year," one of her neighbors said. That was an understatement.

My mother and I had settled into a relationship of mutual responsibility. She was worried about me and how I was recovering. I finally allowed myself to accept her care. And I was worried about her, on her own, miles away, grieving her husband of forty years and living in a huge house on her own. I'd call her every day, not to talk but to make sure she hadn't fallen or the house hadn't exploded. I hated that I couldn't really take care of her from this far away. And that so much of my energy was focused on my health.

As anyone who has been diagnosed with cancer knows, even once you've "beaten" it, you are always on the lookout for its recurrence. My new normal included a routine of additional scans and doctor visits. I was to have a CT scan every six months to rule out any new kidney cancer, and I was also introduced to a nephrologist, whose job it was to keep my remaining kidney healthy. My nephrologist and my urologists seemed to be on speed dial.

In May, it was time for my first sixth-month checkup. Dr. Bradford, my urologist, remarked that my PSA (prostate-specific antigen) was a little high. Actually, for a man in his early forties, it was high enough to be a concern. In addition, my CT scans showed a slightly enlarged prostate. I have always wondered how they measured that. We didn't know what size it was before that scan, so what did "slightly enlarged" mean?

Dr. Bradford didn't want me to be too alarmed. He proposed that I might have an infection and prescribed a course of antibiotics. None of my numbers improved. His next suggestion was a prostate biopsy.

I was wary about undergoing any biopsy. My father had just passed away after an unnecessary biopsy on his lungs. I had not experienced one during my previous diagnosis, and the procedure sounded pretty invasive. But I knew it was the best way forward. We were hoping everything would be clear and I could go on my merry way for another six months. Then I would begin my next cycle of searching for cancer. But searching for cancer was much better than living with cancer.

The day of the biopsy, Lissa drove me to the office because I wouldn't be able to drive myself home. We sat together in the waiting room, flipping through magazines, making small talk. It seemed like we were just there.

When it was time for the procedure, I chatted with the nurse,

Kaky, as I waited for things to start. It turned out that she was a neighbor of a colleague of mine. It was odd having a casual conversation in a setting where I was waiting to be violated for this biopsy.

It didn't take long and then I was on my way home. But I can't say it was an easy process. Yet again I felt like the doctors were minimizing what each procedure would be like. Was I just a wimp or did they minimize the process because otherwise no man in his right mind would submit to it?

It wasn't until a year later, when a coworker pulled a red Swingline stapler out of her desk, that I realized this mundane desk tool offered the perfect way to describe that procedure.

How to Perform a Prostate Biopsy

After the patient is on his side, apply some medical K-Y and make chitchat.

Step 1: Take a Swingline stapler and open it.

Step 2: Insert the stapler into the patient's rectum. Jimmy it around. (There's an ultrasound device in the stapler for navigation.)

Step 3: Dispense one staple into the wall of the rectum close to the prostate area. This first staple will have the local anesthetic.

The sound will make the patient jump off the table. You should steady him with one hand on his hip. Don't let him run away at this point.

Step 4: *Continue to use the stapler until you have twelve prostate samples.*

In addition to the difficult procedure, when Nurse Kaky reviewed my post-op instructions, she said I should expect to see some blood in my urine for a couple of days. (*Haven't I been down this road before?* I thought.) I'd also have rose-colored semen for about a month, "unless you go at it like rabbits."

Okay. Thanks.

When you get to the end of your rope,
tie a knot and hang on. —American proverb

Once again we waited for a few days to receive the results only to discover that the data was decidedly inconclusive. Most of my samples were clear, but there were some ASAP (atypical small acinar proliferation) cells. These cells weren't cancerous, but the results warranted another biopsy. Yippee!

I waited three months to heal up and went through this process again, with two exceptions. Dr. Bradford pulled twenty samples, and I insisted on some type of sedative.

By this time it was August, the end of the summer. Despite the uncertainty about my health, we'd done our best to enjoy some family vacations and logged countless hours at the pool. We tried to pretend everything was normal. We were hoping we could continue that way indefinitely.

We once again sat in Dr. Bradford's office, a place that was becoming uncomfortably familiar. One of the nurses gave me a questionnaire to fill out. The questionnaire had multiple questions about my urological and sexual health. Why would they have me fill out this survey? I knew I had cancer. I just wasn't sure how bad it was. I wondered if Lissa thought the same thing as she watched me complete the form.

In came the doctor. He opened my file.

The news wasn't *too* bad. (Oh, how our gauge of good and bad news gets thrown off during a cancer fight!) Most of the samples were clear. One sample had cancerous cells. They appeared to be slow growing, and since we had taken thirty-two samples between the two biopsies, it was likely a very small cancer.

"So, the kidney cancer has spread?" I asked, confused. I wanted to understand exactly what we were dealing with.

Dr. Bradford shook his head. The area of atypical cells was too far from the kidney. This was prostate cancer.

My eyes widened. I had cancer again. But it wasn't even a spread of my previous cancer. This was a totally new cancer. What in the hell was wrong with me?

Dr. Bradford handed over a stack of papers. "I know you'll want to read, and here are some good places to start." There were a number of treatment options I could pursue. We would set up appointments with the appropriate new doctors and evaluate.

I held the papers tightly as we walked out to the car in silence. I had tried to put on a brave face in the doctor's office, to receive his news with a can-do attitude and a smile. So he knew I was ready to fight again.

Then Lissa and I reached our van. I sat in the passenger seat and Lissa couldn't bring herself to put the key in the ignition. A single tear rolled down my right cheek.

Lissa grabbed my hand. I shook my head. I couldn't even look at her.

"I'm sorry, Lissa, but I wasn't ready for this. I am really disappointed."

I felt her squeeze my hand. I knew this was breaking her heart too.

There was no other way to put it. It was time to go back into battle. But I wasn't feeling like a warrior. I wasn't battle ready. I hadn't recuperated from the previous fight.

How could I utter these words to Emma?

That night I sat down with Emma. It was quiet and our day was winding down. I had to somehow explain that I had cancer again. But while doing so, I had to discuss the prostate, not something I was anxious to do with my thirteen-year-old. I was nervous and screwed up. I told her I had cancer again. I should have started the conversation with "I am okay. I am not in immediate danger." Emma is a smart kid. She heard the word "cancer" and immediately skipped ahead. She started to tear up, and I held her tightly. I was still learning how to talk to her about cancer.

I tried to explain that there really wasn't much cancer there. The prostate was about the size of a walnut and only a tiny proportion of cells were problematic. I wanted to be able to describe the biopsy process and what we'd discovered. The prostate was like a big bowl of popcorn, I told her. The popcorn kernels represent normal, healthy prostate cells. Imagine if there were some M&M's thrown into the bowl. When they performed the first biopsy, they didn't get any M&M's, just popcorn, but they could tell there was some chocolate somewhere in the bowl. In the second biopsy, they actually got an M&M, so they knew what they were dealing with. But really . . . I was mostly just popcorn. Not many M&M's at all.

It was not a perfect analogy. I think I might have confused her more than clarified things.

I reiterated that the doctor was pretty sure I wasn't in immediate danger and that many men develop some type of prostate cancer as they get older. I explained there were various types of treatment we would look into. I would do everything I needed to do to battle and win. We hugged.

Finally, she looked at me and said, "You deserve to be done with this."

I couldn't have agreed more.

Don't eat ice cream unless it's your favorite flavor.

I know this is a hard one for you to accept. You love dessert. You especially love ice cream. I love ice cream. I understand you. It's wonderfully smooth and cold and feeds your soul. I get it. One cup of our favorite ice cream is probably about five hundred calories. Even if it's only four hundred calories, that's a lot of crud to be putting into our bodies. You know me. How often do I take you and Mom to Gelati Celesti and walk out empty-handed? It's more often than not. I will only eat my favorite flavors. I won't waste my calories on a flavor I just like. I have to love it.

Risk something or forever sit with your dreams.
—Herb Brooks

CHAPTER 9

Ready. Fire! Aim.

I sat looking at the phrase I had just written in black pen on Emma's napkin. It was the first day of school and my practice was picking up again. Every now and then I would still have the opportunity to write napkins for Emma during the summer. I looked for every opportunity. Sometimes she attended day camp, where she still needed a packed lunch. If she was headed to a softball practice, I taped one to her water bottle or sneaked it into her backpack. But it was never the same as the consistent, everyday routine of the school year.

Emma was just about to start seventh grade. She was growing

up so fast. But the note I'd written that morning, though it was something that would benefit her, was really written for me. Not feeling ready for battle was an unfamiliar feeling. I've always been someone who takes action. Whether it was pursuing Lissa, looking for that next job opportunity, making sure my daughter has the best education and the healthiest lunch, I am a doer. In fact, I notoriously change the phrase "Ready, aim, fire!" because I think we sometimes spend too much time aiming. Making sure everything is perfectly aligned. When what we really need to do is just act.

I've lived my life being open to opportunities and always looking for a new door to go through. I will often say yes to something that I have *no* business saying yes to. But if you are always saying no, you're always going to miss out on opportunities. Some of the best things that have happened to me haven't been planned but have happened because I was open to saying yes.

My cancer battle was the same way. Each of my doctors knew that I wanted to pursue the most aggressive treatment. And I wanted them to keep looking for the next thing that could work. If there was an ounce of passivity in a doctor, I would find someone else. I needed a warrior, someone leading me into battle, inspiring me to take charge.

There have been very few times in my life when I regretted this aspect about myself. I distinctly remember one.

I always tell my employees to interview all the time, even if they are happy at their current jobs. Interviewing is a learned skill. The only way you get better at it is if you do it. The only way you do it is if you apply for jobs. Or at least respond to interests that come your way. Anytime a recruiter reached out to me to ask if I was looking for a new job, I would say, "No. But I'm listening." In other words, I'm open to opportunities that come my way.

Shortly after Emma was born, I began listening for other job opportunities. As luck would have it, there was an opening at the Staples company. Staples is located outside of Boston, and I'd always hoped for the chance to move back to that area. I loved Lissa and our life in Richmond, but I was far from my family and never really imagined we would settle permanently there. I wasn't sure how Lissa would feel about uprooting our new family to move to New England, but I was just going to interview. We could face the decision if a job offer presented itself.

My phone interview with the hiring manager was scheduled for a Sunday evening. It was a fantastic interview that lasted over an hour and a half. We spoke at length about retail practices, the challenges both Circuit City and Staples faced in the marketplace, the work environment at Staples, and we even took the time to discuss our personal motivations. I loved her management style.

I wasn't surprised to receive a call the next day from the HR department asking if I could fly up for some further interviews. They were trying to book a flight for me for that Wednesday. It would be a quick turnaround. I'd fly up in the morning, meet with a handful of the merchant team, have lunch with the hiring manager, complete some more interviews, and then fly back to Richmond early that evening. I was excited.

I started planting the seed at work that I wouldn't be coming into work on Wednesday. My coworkers always joked whenever someone showed up at work in a suit. The assumption was that this person was interviewing elsewhere. It didn't happen often, but I had seen it enough that I knew a suit could arouse suspicion. I was a little nervous about taking the day off, unplanned, but at least I would be in a different city and my coworkers would be in Richmond.

As I worked through Tuesday, I noticed that there was an unusually high level of activity for a couple of people on my team. Blaine was my boss's manager, and he and Danny Bird, my coworker, were running around like crazy. Out of curiosity, I asked someone else what was happening. "Oh, they're headed up to Boston tomorrow for a last-minute meeting with Road Runner," came the reply.

Uh-oh. This could certainly add a wrinkle to my travel plans. The Richmond airport wasn't that large. There were only so many flights to and from Boston. I was sure to run into them.

I needed to find out their travel details. I decided to go straight to Danny and ask what he was doing the next day. When he talked about their plans to fly up to Boston for the day, I sheepishly admitted I had similar travel plans and was somewhat concerned about running into Blaine during my travels. Danny and I compared our itineraries. Thankfully, our morning flights were about twenty minutes apart and the gates were separated enough I was relatively confident I'd be able to avoid the two of them.

However, we were on the same exact return flight Wednesday evening. This was going to be a disastrous interview day. I was suddenly very nervous.

I woke up early on Wednesday and headed off to the airport. And while I didn't see Blaine or Danny, I also didn't see the inside of my flight. My flight was delayed . . . and delayed . . . and delayed.

I called the team at Staples to let them know that I was severely delayed, and they adjusted my interview schedule. When I finally arrived in Boston, they had a shuttle van waiting for me, and I rode out to Framingham. It was so late I had missed the morning interviews planned for me. I was brought to the cafeteria and wolfed down something to eat. I was ready to start.

As we walked to my first interview, I explained my predicament to the HR rep, that I would be on the same flight back to Richmond as my boss, and I wanted to avoid that at all costs. She chuckled a bit and assured me that Staples would do their best to get me back to the airport earlier than originally planned and booked on an earlier flight.

The in-person interviews were even better than my phone interview. I was pretty sure I wanted this job. I would just have to convince Lissa this was a good move for us. She had always loved visiting me in Boston, but she had never really experienced a New England winter. That could be our biggest challenge.

Once the interviews were complete, I rushed back to the airport. Staples had rebooked my flight and I was all set to leave. My hopes fell as I walked into the terminal. Every flight in the mid-Atlantic region was delayed. What was going on? There were massive thunderstorms from New York City down through Virginia. All the flights were running late, and worse yet, my flight was canceled! Yes, you guessed it. I was automatically rebooked on my original flight and would be on the same plane as Blaine and Danny. I couldn't believe this. *I am so fired*, I kept thinking.

I paced around the terminal for a few minutes and wondered what to do. What would my boss think if he ran into me up here? I couldn't afford to be fired! I had a new baby at home! I was starting to question why I'd even interviewed for this job. Wasn't my current job good enough? Why was I always looking for something better? Why did I say yes to this? I was quickly working myself into a frenzy.

I decided to call Lissa. I apologized to her for putting us in this crazy situation and asked her what I should do. As I was listening to her try to calm me down, assuring me everything was going to be okay, Blaine and Danny walked right in front of me. My heart stopped. But they kept walking. They never even noticed I was there. I was thankful I was dressed like every other businessman in the airport, but I knew that wouldn't last long. As soon as I was at our gate, they would see me.

Suddenly, I realized what I had to do. I hung up with Lissa, hopped the T, and rode into Boston. I walked into a Champs Sports store and after a few minutes purchased shorts, sneakers, a baseball cap, and a Patriots T-shirt. I stuffed my suit into the shopping bag and made my way back to the airport. Then I bought a copy of *The Boston Globe* newspaper. It was a wide newspaper and, when opened, could easily conceal me. At the very least I was dressed in street clothes and could explain away being in Boston for personal reasons if I were caught.

As I sat pretending to read my *Boston Globe*, my mind was still spinning. I decided I needed help. I walked up to the check-in counter and told my story to the two guys working there. They laughed at my situation. "And I bet you called in sick so you could come up here, didn't you? You are so fired!" One of them said. They clearly saw humor in this day, but I wasn't finding it quite as funny.

Finally, they stopped laughing and one asked, "So, why are you telling us this?" I explained that I needed some help getting out of this tight spot. I had an idea. I wanted to be a passenger "needing special assistance boarding." I was in the very last row of the plane. If I boarded first, I could slink back to the last row and sit inconspicuously. I'd get on the plane first and leave last. If the guys at the gate would help me, I might just make it home without being seen.

The two of them were happy to help. One even mentioned that he would open the door to the Jetway and wave me through even before they made the announcement regarding passengers needing special assistance! I was finally safe!

I sat back down and began the wait. The two guys at the counter kept looking at me from time to time and chuckling. As I glanced up another time, they waved me over again. I stood cautiously and looked around the gate area. There was no sign of Blaine or Danny. I was still in the clear. I walked up to the counter.

"Okay, Mr. Callaghan," the agent said. "Your plan is good. You can get on the plane first and leave last, *or* you can get on the plane last and leave first." I wasn't fully comprehending what he was stating until he handed me a first-class upgrade ticket. I was now seated in seat 1B. I could literally walk on last, well after Blaine and Danny would be in their seats. Once we landed, I would rush out and be well ahead of them. What a gift!

I was just about to start my third hour in the airport. I had read every article in the paper, but hadn't seen Blaine or Danny again. They were probably grabbing something to eat. The two at the counter were still chuckling now and then. Once more, one of them waved me up. I thought, *What else could possibly happen?*

He mentioned that flights were still very delayed and many were being canceled. I stood there thinking he was telling me I wouldn't make it home. Instead, he asked me what my boss's name was. I started to explain that Blaine was actually my boss's boss, but I realized he didn't need that level of detail. "Blaine Altaffer is my boss." His fingers danced furiously on the keyboard. The other gate agent leaned over and asked, "What are you doing?" He replied that the weather was still impacting flights and that Mr. Altaffer was about to get bumped. This was incredible! I couldn't believe this. Not only had they helped me out, giving me a first-class upgrade, but they also were going to bump Blaine in order to help keep me safe! What a day!

I made it home safely, undiscovered.*

---

* Postscript: It turns out that Blaine got impatient and was already on a flight to Norfolk. He must have planned to drive back to Richmond from that airport. I did receive the Staples job offer a few days later. Although I was really excited about the job, I didn't accept it. It wasn't the right move for my family at the time. To the best of my knowledge, Blaine never found out about my trip. I was always fearful of telling him. I didn't think he'd see the humor in what happened. To this day, I still have that Patriots T-shirt. I consider it my very first "lucky" shirt.

Make stepping-stones out of stumbling blocks.
—Unknown

I smile as I remember this ridiculous moment in my life, when I was really afraid that I'd messed everything up and was about to be fired. In that moment, I didn't feel like my can-do, make-it-work, pursue-it-all personality was an asset; it felt like a liability. But it all worked out. Things always worked out. Why couldn't I remember that as I faced cancer? Remember how blessed my life had been? Have faith that there was a path ahead for me, a treatment that would address this?

A couple of days later I was headed in for another doctor visit. Unfortunately, I soon found out that with this battle with cancer, it wouldn't be so clear how best to "attack."

Don't do drugs.

This isn't an option. There are enough legal substances (not including air, water, and food) that you can put into your body to alter your perception of reality; you don't have to try things that are illegal. It's just not safe. Most won't kill you. I admit that. However, there is no compelling reason a smart, poised, graceful, and awesome girl like you needs to try drugs. They absolutely won't make you more awesome. You shouldn't do it, nor should you allow someone else to.

Your life will ultimately be determined by the choices you make. Choose wisely. I don't really have a story to put here. This is just plain fatherly advice.

Do not pray for an easy life, pray for the strength to endure a difficult one.
—Bruce Lee

CHAPTER 10

Active Surveillance

I stumbled upon this quote a few weeks after my prostate diagnosis and had set it aside for one of Emma's notes. This morning I knew it was appropriate for all of us. Obviously, we were being dealt a difficult hand right now. We all needed strength and perspective to know how to endure this with grace and dignity, and with our family intact.

It was time to go in and establish a plan. Just a few weeks after my initial diagnosis, in mid-September, I headed back to the hospital to meet with specialists. Dr. Bradford had explained that there were five types of therapy to consider.

We immediately ruled out the first option—hormone therapy—since I was young.

I met with a radiation oncologist to discuss the two radiation options and my health history at length. She was really concerned that I had been diagnosed with both kidney cancer and prostate cancer at such a young age (*You and me both*, I thought). She asked me about my family and any risk factors I knew of. I described my environment growing up and even admitted to breaking a thermometer as a child and playing with the mercury. She didn't say this was a risk factor. (I am sorry, Mom. I don't know that I ever confessed to this!) She did take note of the time that I lived in West Germany as an exchange student. On April 26, 1986, the Chernobyl nuclear reactor melted down and released a significant amount of radiation. I was living in Germany at this time and remember everyone being concerned about the fruits and vegetables we ate. I was caught in a rainstorm shortly after this disaster, and my host family practically stripped me down and threw me into the shower. The doctor made a special note of this but didn't know if there was anything we could act upon.

When we were wrapping up, I decided to be straightforward. I looked her in the eye and asked, "Is there something wrong with me?" She closed up my file and sighed. "Yes, most likely." She couldn't say what, but there was clearly something that was making me predisposed to these two cancers. She urged me to be proactive and watch for symptoms of bladder and testicular cancer. She practically begged me to choose to undergo surgery as soon as possible.

Surgery was the fourth option. I could have a prostatectomy, which would remove my prostate. The hope was that all the cancerous cells, as well as the healthy cells, would be taken out. The entire gland would be removed.

This was presented as the most viable course of action. But as I pushed further, asked my doctor more questions, I realized he was glossing over the vast, and hugely impactful, side effects. I was discovering that there are a lot of things doctors don't talk about that are *very* distressing for men.

Here are a few choice side effects I would likely experience if I decided to undergo a prostatectomy:

- *nerve damage, leading to an inability to experience erections*
- *incontinence*
- *changes in orgasm, including a lack of ejaculation (The prostate produces semen, which would no longer exist.)*

- *shrinkage (Yes, you read that right: shrinkage! The procedure cuts the urethra during the prostate removal and it is then reattached. Some men claim this impacts them in a very negative manner.)*

Um, seriously? I was supposed to just sign up for all of that at the age of forty-three?

The average age of prostate diagnosis is sixty-nine. When you are almost seventy, dealing with those side effects would be unfortunate but probably worth it to minimize the risk of the cancer spreading. You may have already been experiencing those side effects as a result of old age. But that was not my reality. I wanted this cancer gone, obviously. But signing up for a lifetime without sex? I wasn't ready for that.

There was one final option Dr. Bradford presented. He believed we might over-treat prostate cancer in the United States, and especially in my case, we could instead enter into "active surveillance." We would continue to monitor my PSA levels every other month, with a follow-up biopsy about a year into the program. In theory, we could continue on this path indefinitely until we saw a spike in PSA levels or a positive result in a biopsy. Although I wasn't looking forward to an annual prostate biopsy, this seemed like an acceptable course of action.

The question was could I live each day knowing that there was cancer inside me? Could I risk this? How would this impact my mental, emotional, and spiritual well-being? What if it started growing uncontrollably and we hadn't caught it in time? Could I ever forgive myself for not being more aggressive, doing everything possible to make sure I was around for Emma? I had just undergone an extensive surgery in order to get cancer out of my body a year ago. It seemed wrong to let this one stick around. It seemed like I was stepping away from the fight.

Lissa and I had time to consider the options. We knew we were deciding between surgery and watching. Ultimately, the surgery had some potential side effects that I, as a forty-three-year-old man, was not willing to risk. We were past the time when I wanted to have more children, but I certainly did not want to risk losing some, if not all, aspects of sex. That thought was truly unthinkable.

As much as it pained me, we decided to enter into active surveillance. I would be walking around every day with cancer in my body. I would know that it was there, a potential time bomb wait-ing to explode and possibly kill me. I had attacked kidney cancer with every possible weapon, and I felt like I was waving the white flag on the battle with prostate cancer.

Cancer didn't win, but at best it was a tie ball game.

LESSON #34:

Put your phone down.

I know. Your phone is a new tool. It's a thing. Yes, it connects you to friends and loved ones. It's a thing. You don't need to be connected all day. Take a break. Be by yourself. Be alone in your thoughts.

When you are with someone else, be present. Pay attention. Listen. Put your phone down. If you can go to the movie theater for a couple of hours and keep your phone in your pocket, you can offer the same courtesy to your family during dinner.

Dear Emma, It's okay to seek help when you need it. Really, ask me. I'm here. Love, Dad

CHAPTER 11

Six Words I Say to Emma

I was introduced to Rachel Macy Stafford, also known as Hands Free Mama, through a blog post called "Six Words You Should Say Today." I immediately developed a deep appreciation for her parenting style.

She'd read an article about how when college athletes are asked what kind of encouragement and advice they most appreciated from their parents, they simply liked the phrase "I like to watch you play." Rachel started to use this phrase with her kids and realized how it immediately lifted the pressure off her kids. She wasn't providing criticism or even feedback. It just focused on the joy watching them play their sport, or instrument, brought her.

The blog post touched me deeply. I also started using her phrase "I love to watch you play" whenever I could. Emma plays softball. Sitting at her games, in the bleachers, as I watch her work together with her teammates brings me more joy than I ever could have imagined possible. Even more these days. As I continued to battle cancer, being at her games took on a deep significance for me. It was not just to watch her, for the joy it brought me to observe her. It was also a tangible way to show her support. To show her how I will always, always be there for her. For as long as I am on this earth.

One night Emma was headed to a sleepover with one of her softball teams. They didn't always get to see one another that much when it was off-season and they wanted to keep their ties. I was excited for her. Her team is made up of incredibly talented girls who are also the best sports in the league. Everyone is lifted higher during their games, even the spectators.

We were warned that the house had a few animals, and Emma can have allergic reactions from time to time. We thought we'd give it a chance. But when Emma started having some trouble early in the evening, we collectively decided that it would be a better idea for Emma to come home.

I left our house at ten P.M. to go fetch her. I was tired. It had been a long day, and I am usually asleep by ten P.M. on a normal day. Rest is important, but not as important as my daughter. I drove the twenty-five minutes, in the dark, without a single thought of my fatigue. I was happy to make this trip.

Emma hopped into my truck as I asked if she was okay. She replied, "I'd never make it the whole night. Thank you for coming to get me."

I looked her in the eye and simply said, *"I will always come get you."* She kind of nodded her head, and I repeated it. *"I will always come get you."* She thought that I believed she hadn't heard me, and she acknowledged my statement. I knew she'd heard me, but I needed her to listen to me.

"I will always come get you."

I held her hand for a moment and let her internalize what I meant. She slowly nodded as she understood. She smiled.

I then listed some of the reasons why I might need to come get her: a flat tire, a bad date, homesickness, or even a friend who had too much to drink and shouldn't get behind the wheel.

"I will always come get you. I am your dad, and I will be there. Call me, no questions asked, at least until you're home safely. I will never say no."

I didn't realize until later that this phrase also had six words in it. And it was just as meaningful as "I love to watch you play."

When I told Emma those words, I was just thinking of her. I was just thinking of how much I loved her and how much I would always be there for her if I had anything to do with it. I've now realized how much that statement equates to how God likely feels about us.

I've been a Catholic all my life. I grew up in an Irish Catholic family, which meant that most celebrations revolved around religious holidays and festivities. They also usually involved lengthy pinochle tournaments and various drinks containing rye whiskey. The pinochle score sheets were preserved from get-together to get-together, because the consumption of the rye would often create false memories of games played. I never acquired a taste for rye, but I can hold my own in a pinochle game or a religious discussion.

Port Leyden was a small town, but we had five churches. Most of the town attended one of the services on Sundays. My first memories of religion are of religious education classes with Sister Mary Agnes. She was a tough-as-nails nun and didn't take any guff. If we learned our prayers and Bible verses, we received a silver star in our catechism books. If we didn't, the punishment could range from a ruler on the knuckles to reading the prayer out loud over and over again. Religious ed. with Sister Mary Agnes was a far cry from Vacation Bible School with craft making, singing, and watered-down Tang punch!

I became an altar boy a couple of years after First Communion and served during Mass. We often had half a dozen altar boys to assist the priest. I felt good helping, but I didn't necessarily feel faithful. My actions seemed trite and relatively inconsequential. It wasn't until Father Mulvaney was transferred to our parish that I truly learned about faith.

Father Mulvaney embodied faith. Every word he spoke came from his heart. He loved God, and it was his calling to teach others about this love. Father Mulvaney was personally responsible for teaching the altar boys why certain actions were important during Mass. My role took on new meaning.

As I approached the sacrament of confirmation, I had to choose a confirmation name. I chose Andrew—not for Saint Andrew, the patron saint of fishermen and rope makers, but for the influence that Father Andrew Mulvaney had on my life. I grew in my faith and belief in God. I joined the music group and became a Eucharistic minister.

Despite the outward appearances, deep down I was too stubborn to believe that God actually played a daily role in my life. I had free will and I was in control of my destiny. Part of my resistance was the fact that I was so decidedly human. I made mistakes. I had bad judgment. I didn't always do the right thing, nor was I always a good person. I was very selfish, especially with my time. I didn't hear God correcting me, but I wasn't listening very closely. As I grew older, I slowly stopped participating in Mass and even skipped some Sundays. Eventually, I couldn't even call myself an armchair Catholic.

As I grew into adulthood, I often joked that I should have chosen Thomas for my confirmation name, as in Doubting Thomas. I did my best to lead my family, but I often stumbled. It wasn't until Emma was ten that she went through the initiation of baptism and First Communion. We joined a FIRE (family-centered intergenerational religious education) group and started attending Mass again.

When I was diagnosed with cancer, I immediately added myself to the prayer list at church. Unfortunately, that was how many of my friends at the church learned about my diagnosis: when my name was listed as one of the people needing prayer for their battle with cancer. I heard the round of gasps as my name was called. I hated that I couldn't tell every person individually, but I had a battle to fight! I had a family to try to keep together!

Before my first surgery, I asked our parish priest to perform an anointing of the sick, one of the seven sacraments. I had never been the recipient of this sacrament and was humbled as the priest tended me, praying over me. I wanted to feel God's presence, be assured that he was looking out for me, but I had my doubts. Yet one thing stood out as I listened to Father Dan talk to God on my behalf. He prayed not just for me to be healed but also for my surgeons, for them to be led by God and do their jobs well.

It was a powerful distinction for me. I hadn't thought about that before. Going into surgery knowing that people were praying for not just me but also the many doctors and nurses in that room attending to me, it was powerful. I guess I had more faith that God could heal me through the doctors than faith that he could heal me on his own.

I was fortunate also that the hospital I frequent is a religious institution. The staff there can choose to wear a button on their uniforms that says "I pray." It was so comforting to have nurses and doctors attending to me, and have a visual reminder that these people put their trust in God as well.

After my surgery, as I was recovering at home, some generous people brought Communion to me, since I couldn't attend Mass myself. But when I was fully recovered, back at work, and had a clean bill of health, I never went back to Mass.

He who does not seek will not find.
—Unknown

When I received a second cancer diagnosis, something changed for me. I was usually fine, until I had time to myself. When I was on my own, I got angry. To be honest, I had felt a rolling boil of anger since the very first day I was diagnosed. Anger that originated as fear. My family's future was at risk. I hadn't figured out how to win this battle. I didn't know enough. And I needed someone to blame.

The second diagnosis caused the anger to truly erupt. It wasn't beneath the surface anymore. I tried to bargain with God. I didn't want Emma to grow up without a father, without me. I would do anything, give up anything, to keep that from happening. Oddly enough, no matter how much rage bubbled within, I still believed in God. I still knew he existed, but I hated him for what he was doing to me. I hated him for Emma's sake.

How could he do this to me? How could he allow this to happen?

Our parish priest, Father Dan, had recently battled prostate cancer. So, when I was diagnosed, I decided to talk to him about his experience. I hoped he would be able to give me some good perspective. I was nervous about seeing him. He knew that our family had been absent lately.

I sat down in his light-filled office. It was the first time I'd really talked to him one-on-one. We talked about my family and how we were handling all of this. We didn't even talk that much about faith per se. But finally he asked me, "Are you angry with God?"

I sat there, staring at my hands. How could he ask me that? If I said no, he would know I was lying. If I said yes, that was blasphemy. There was no way to win.

He could see the struggle going on within me. I shifted in my seat. Just as I was about to lie and say no, he spoke up. "It's okay if you are. He has big enough shoulders to handle that."

A dam broke within me and I just started crying, tears coursing down my cheeks. I was grateful for being allowed to feel what I was feeling. To have someone like Father Dan tell me that it was okay.

I'd been trying so hard to keep it together. My emotions. My fears. My family. My health.

And I'd been ashamed to be angry with God. And so I hadn't been giving him any of my burden. I'd just been carrying it myself. And drowning under the weight.

It meant so much to be given permission to struggle with God. To be reminded that just as I will always be there for Emma, no matter what she has done, just as her actions will never cause me to love her any less, God feels that way about us. The dark times we experience in life are not because God has left but because we've turned away.

And the joy he experiences when we turn back is . . . unimaginable.

Things are things.

You should love people. You should even love your pets. You can love experiences with people. Don't love things. Things can be replaced if they are broken or damaged. People can't.

We were financially struggling last year. The medical bills were piling up. I kept getting diagnosed with cancer, and there wasn't an end in sight. I wasn't sure if I was going to be able to pay our mortgage. I looked around my home office and saw things. Some were very special. Yes, I might even say I loved having them. I saw limited edition Star Wars LEGOs, a Boba Fett limited edition figure (one of two hundred and fifty!), my Sony PSP, which I'd purchased on its release date (I was the first person in line!), a laptop, and my iPad. I sold them all. I didn't think twice. Things are things.

> The two most important days in your life are the day you are born and the day you find out why. —Mark Twain

CHAPTER 12

Feeling the Call

Ever since I had seen how Emma collected my notes in her composition book, I considered sharing my practice with some of my online social networks. I thought maybe I could show other parents how easy it was to connect daily with their children, despite their busy schedules, and how this very little thing had seemed to really mean something to Emma. But I was hesitant. I wasn't doing anything remarkable. I knew many parents had a practice of writing something on a napkin if they packed their kids' lunches.

I was especially interested in inspiring dads to make lunches and include a special note. As a full-time working dad, I struggled with the fact that my wife spent so much more time with Emma. Napkin Notes had become my thing. A special thing I shared with my daughter. That connected us. I thought maybe other dads might like the idea.

These ideas had been percolating for months, but I never did anything. I had my hands full with work, family life, my health. Before we knew it, Christmas season was upon us. It had been almost five months since we'd decided to "live" with this cancer inside me. I hated that another Christmas season was tainted by the shadow of my diagnosis. But we were thankful to be together, and we celebrated like any other year. Except for the gift Lissa gave me.

I had seen the large box sitting perfectly wrapped under the Christmas tree. I was anxious with anticipation, wondering what she'd gotten me this year. Finally, it was my turn, and Lissa walked over with the big box, a huge smile on her face.

I tore into it. I'm not one to save paper. I think the bigger the mess on Christmas morning, the better. And there it was. An Xbox 360.

I started to cry. I was immediately struck with two thoughts.

First, I knew how much Lissa had sacrificed, going to a store and purchasing a video game system. She's not a technology lover like myself. I knew the conversations with salespeople about which gaming system was right for me must have been painful. Lissa doesn't see the appeal in playing most video games and finds my fascination with digital entertainment a bit bothersome. I have, in the past, spent way too much time playing on my PC or console.

Second, because of her predisposition against electronics and video games, I honestly thought, for a few seconds, that she had possibly intercepted a call from my doctor and knew that I was dying. I mean, why else would she want to give me a game system unless it was the end of my days?

Needless to say, I was overjoyed with the gift.

When I started playing Halo, my nightmares stopped. Immediately. They didn't dwindle down. They didn't slowly become less violent. They disappeared. Overnight. The nightmares that had been plaguing me for over a year, often causing me to get up at three in the morning so as not to be subjected to them anymore, they vanished.

A great Christmas coupled with the disappearance of my nightmares finally put me in the right frame of mind to actually start sharing some of my Napkin Notes online. I thought simply sharing the quotes I wrote to Emma each day might be helpful to someone. Plus, it was something positive to focus on. For the last two years, I'd been mired in cancer statistics, MRIs, blood tests. Instead of fighting something evil, I wanted to create something good.

I started slowly. I didn't even really say what I was doing. I just posted a quote and started the post with "180NN"—"180" was the total number of school days left that I would write notes for Emma each school year; 180 opportunities remained to inspire, shape, mold. "NN" stood for Napkin Notes. So, two days after Christmas I posted:

We either make ourselves miserable, or we make ourselves strong. The amount of work is the same. —Carlos Castaneda

---

I sporadically shared thoughts and notes online over the next few weeks. I created a slogan: "Pack. Write. Connect." I felt that captured what it was I was trying to do. Pack a lunch. Write a note. Connect with my kid.

I kept it simple. To show people how easy it was to do something small that could have a big meaning.

By the summer, a few coworkers mentioned they were following my posts. With their feedback, I decided to start an "official" Napkin Notes page on Facebook. The first picture posted was a photograph of the Napkin Note I'd written to Emma for the last day of school.

You alone are enough. You have nothing to prove to anybody. —Maya Angelou

---

Then something remarkable happened.

I was having lunch with someone I had never met before. David Brumfield was a recruiter, and I was interested in talking to him about some job opportunities. He and I were discussing how we spend our time before our respective families wake up. I mentioned that I was typically the primary lunch maker for my daughter and often spent time researching quotes to pack in her lunch. I shared how I felt a connection with Emma as I prepared for her both the food and the note. He replied, "Oh, like

Napkin Notes. I have been following them on Facebook."

I looked at him hard. Was he kidding? Nope. He wasn't. He had no idea that I was the Napkin Note guy.

Flabbergasted, I laughed and said, "Dude, I'm that guy. Napkin Notes is my Facebook page."

He couldn't believe it. We continued talking about how important it was for dads to connect with their children and how this was a great way to connect.

As we finished lunch, David asked me to walk with him to his car. He looked at me and said, "I just wanted you to see that I really do this." He pulled out a lunch box from the backseat, opened it, and showed me the note he had included for his daughter the day before. It was the exact note I had posted on Facebook a few days prior: "I love you. Make today awesome."

I was flooded with a number of emotions. I was humbled. Here it was. This was what I had hoped for. And it had actually happened. I had inspired someone to connect with his kid.

I left that lunch on cloud nine.

How did David and I get connected? What was at work here? He and I had not met until that day. Our conversation was incredibly casual, and the only reason we had started discussing Napkin

Notes was that I'd mentioned getting up early in the morning to work on a personal project.

A few close friends and colleagues had occasionally commented that God was working through me. I didn't quite comprehend what that meant. I was just writing Napkin Notes for Emma and sharing them. I am certainly not a model parent or husband. I make my share of mistakes, and I suffer the same human frailties as everyone else. I didn't feel holy or spiritual doing this. I wasn't even practicing my religion!

My wife wasn't raised Catholic but has been a huge supporter of the spiritual life of our family. She noticed all the Sundays that had passed without our attending Mass. I could tell she was giving me the space to determine when I was ready to go back.

I never would have guessed that it would be Emma who initiated our return.

There was a boy from school I had noticed Emma was drawn to at a few different picnics and social gatherings we'd attended together. It was probably about time for her to show a real interest in boys. I wasn't excited to be entering that phase of fatherhood, but there was also a part of me that was touched to see that side of my growing daughter.

I didn't know much about this boy, but I knew he attended a different Catholic church in our town. It became clear that Emma had developed a true crush when she casually asked to attend Mass at his church.

I smiled and tried not to let her know that I understood what was really going on. And I said yes, of course we could go to Mass at St. Mary's.

I was thankful for my conversation with Father Dan. Knowing that God could handle my anger helped me show my face at church without feeling like a hypocrite. I sat and listened to the gospel, Emma nestled by my side, craning her neck to see if her "friend" was here. The gospel was Matthew 4:12-23. I listened closely to the story about Jesus walking along the Sea of Galilee, calling his disciples away from their lives, and how they followed without question. I'd never felt like a true disciple. If God was calling me, I seemed to always be dragging my feet.

I had felt a lightness in my spirit since handing over my burdens to God. As I sat in the pew, hearing the sermon, I tried to listen in, to see if God was speaking to me. Where might God be trying to lead me?

Don't sleep around.

Respect yourself. Respect your loved one. I would love to think you will someday fall in love with The One and be with that person for the rest of your life. I am sure you want to believe that too. Sex is supposed to be fun, but you need to value yourself and your body. Better yet, you need to love someone who loves and respects you.

I want you to love. I want you to have the self-confidence to respect your body and soul. Stay in control.

Round Three

Life doesn't have to be perfect to be wonderful.

—ANNETTE FUNICELLO

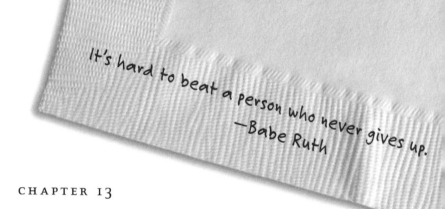

It's hard to beat a person who never gives up.
—Babe Ruth

CHAPTER 13

Whac-A-Mole (or I'm Tired of Making Emma Cry)

I wiped away a tear as I slowly folded the napkin. Sometimes I found myself drawn to quotes that I needed to hear, that I needed to believe, when packing Emma's lunch and writing her napkins. The tears were present because in the dark of dawn, I knew I felt like giving up.

I have cancer again.

I have cancer again.

I have cancer again.

The words reverberated in my head like a racquetball, bouncing against my skull, each time hitting harder.

I'd gone in for my routine scan in late September and had a biopsy the same day. The scan would determine whether we were having any kidney "issues" and the biopsy was to assess any growth from my prostate cancer. I was a few months late for my checkup. But I'd been waiting until I'd paid off some of my previous bills before I racked up even more. Now it was finally time to assess whether our active surveillance was working.

My CT scan revealed some "vague" areas. I hated vague. Vague always meant more tests. The doctors recommended an MRI. By this time, I knew the drill. I lay in the tube, listening to the bumps and whirs. I didn't expect a call the next day since the MRI had been done at eight o'clock at night. However, my doctor called at ten A.M. to report once again that I had cancer.

"There's something on your adrenal gland," he said. "We could go in and biopsy it or just go in and take it out. You have two adrenal glands so you don't really need this one. Because of how close your adrenal glands are to your kidney, it's safe to assume that it's your kidney cancer that has spread."

The doctor made sure I had his cell phone number in case I wanted to talk about anything.

Oh cool, I have all my doctors' cell phone numbers, I thought. And then

I thought, *Oh shit, I have all my doctors' cell phone numbers.*

But I ended the phone call with, "Let's do it. Schedule the surgery. Let's rock!"

My doctor said, "Mr. Callaghan, I knew you'd say that."

I leaned back in my desk chair and stared blankly at the wall. We had just started another school year and here we were again. Another fall, another cancer.

Our family had been on such a high this week. Our local paper, the *Richmond Times-Dispatch*, had done a feature on Napkin Notes. I was hugely touched by their interest and even more so when I saw the actual story. It covered most of the front page of the life and leisure section and continued on the inside! They even had a little blurb about it on the front page of the newspaper. It was an embarrassment of riches and a blip of light that we'd so needed as a family. I hated what all of this had done to Emma, that she'd had to talk to a reporter about what it might be like to one day lose me, and yet if it encouraged other families to connect in deeper ways, maybe all of this was worth it.

But then why was I facing cancer yet again?

It took me two days to work up the courage to tell Emma. When I finally sat down with her, I kept hoping she'd somehow bring up a question about sex so I wouldn't have to tell her. Sadly, I didn't get to go into my spiel about human reproduction. Instead, I had to tell her that I had cancer again. I held her tightly in my lap, so I couldn't see if she was crying. My voice wavered a bit, but I managed to start talking about Chuck E. Cheese's and the Whac-A-Mole game. I explained that my cancer might just keep popping up from time to time, and we'd just whack it back down, like the mole.

She paused and then said, "But you can't win Whac-A-Mole. You're going to win this."

God bless that child.

Life is too short to work for a jerk.

I once worked for a company as a district manager and managed a handful of stores. The company was based in Virginia Beach. I only went into the corporate office a few times a month. I always had this sneaking suspicion that something was wrong there. Every time I hired a new employee, their first question was "Is he black?" What? We weren't living in 1960! I overheard two coworkers talking about potentially suing because they were being discriminated against. They were pregnant. I also found out that I was considered a stick-in-the-mud because I didn't partake in the company drug parties.

Needless to say, I left that company and didn't look back.

Work is important to me. I think it will be important to you. You'll probably have a few bosses and managers in your life. Your life is too short to work for a jerk.

> *Be a rainbow in someone else's cloud.*
> —Maya Angelou

CHAPTER 14

The Every Day Action Hero

During prep for my surgery, one of the nurses asked the routine question, "Do you understand the risks and benefits of this procedure?" What can I say? At this point I had a sense of humor about it all.

"Yes," I said. "The risk is I die, and the benefit is I get to live."

I don't think they were quite prepared for that.

Recovery was a piece of cake this time. I didn't even end up filling my prescription for the pain medication. But when the pathology came back two weeks later, it wasn't good news. The cancer wasn't fully removed. It was still in my body. I was officially placed in the high-risk category.

I couldn't pretend anymore. This was it. I was going to die. It was on the horizon. I wasn't sure how far away, but I could see it.

We were hoping to get into some experimental trials for kidney cancer. I was really focused on getting an appointment at MD Anderson in Houston. When I'd been diagnosed the first time with kidney cancer, through all my research, I had compiled an extensive list of the best programs and hospitals. I went straight back to that list and MD Anderson was at the top. But they wanted a thousand-dollar deposit in order to secure a slot on their schedule. I didn't have a thousand dollars sitting around. But by January they would be in my insurance network. We would just have to wait.

A few days after surgery, I was headed to Orlando for a job interview. (You can fill a guy with cancer, but you can't change his stripes! I was still open to pursuing different opportunities for work, always hoping to secure the best possible future for Lissa and Emma no matter what happened to me.) I sat in my seat, waiting for the plane to take off, wanting to quell the thoughts racing in my mind. I shifted in my seat, stretching my legs. I'd brought a book, but it wasn't capturing my attention. I looked through the magazines in the pocket of the seat in front of me, found the Southwest Airlines' *Spirit* magazine, and started flipping through it.

An article caught my attention. It was titled "The Every Day Action Hero." Of course, being the Star Wars geek that I am, I was interested. I started reading. And started crying.

It was the story of Alex Sheen, a young man who had started a social movement about the power of keeping a promise after the death of his father. Because I Said I Would (Becauseisaidiwould.com) encouraged people to follow through on their intentions. The one thing Alex remembered about his dad was that he always kept his promises. No matter what. He was a man of his word. Alex realized how little that commitment was valued in our quick-to-move-on society. He wanted to refocus people, and himself, on doing what we say we will do. He created small business cards that he would mail out to people who wanted to make a promise. At the bottom of the blank card it simply said "because I said I would." People would write their commitment at the top, take a photo of the card, and post it online.

Some of the promises were little. Some of them were huge.

Obviously, I was in a fragile space. Facing another diagnosis that looked grim at best. Facing the fact that the doctor had said patients like me had about an 8 percent five-year survival rate. Emma would graduate high school in four and a half years. There was a very good chance I wouldn't be there to write a Napkin Note for Emma every day until she graduated from high school.

I knew that there was an implied promise to Emma that I'd always pack her lunch and write a Napkin Note for her. But that possibility seemed to be slipping away. What was I going to do?

There was so little I could control in this battle. I didn't understand why I was having to continue to fight when many men reached their seventies without any significant health issues. They got to watch their kids not only graduate from high school but also graduate college, get jobs, get married.

But making sure Emma always had a Napkin Note? That was something I could control.

I vowed right then and there, in seat 34B, that I would write out as many Napkin Notes as I needed to in order for her to have one every school day until she graduated. I quickly estimated how many Napkin Notes I would need to last through graduation and set out to write, write, write as soon as I got home: 826. 826 notes to write to be able to fulfill this promise to my daughter.

Once I landed, before I even checked into my hotel, I e-mailed Alex, told him about how the article had inspired me and the promise I was going to make. A few days later he actually responded. He was inspired by my commitment to Emma and the Napkin Notes. I was shocked. Alex's mission was big. He was doing great things. I was just a dad with cancer writing out Napkin Notes.

Coming in contact with Alex and his mission did something for me. It helped me focus. Rather than focus on the grim prognosis I had just received, it made me focus on what I was going to leave behind. And, by golly, I was going to give my girl every piece of advice she may need in life.

If you can't talk about it, you shouldn't do it.

Would you ask me advice on how to cheat on a test? How about robbing a bank? If the hair on the back of your neck stands up when you think about that conversation, you shouldn't do it.

Could you easily ask your best friend if you could date her boyfriend? I didn't think so.

You're mature enough to have adult conversations about actions, feelings, and thoughts. Have those conversations. If you can't, then maybe you aren't mature enough to commit that action.

> What you do today can change all the tomorrows of your life. —Zig Ziglar

CHAPTER 15

The Best Christmas Present Ever

Lissa had long been after me to visit the oncology department of VCU Massey Cancer Center. She'd heard great things, they were in our insurance network, and they were located right here in Richmond. They'd be able to meet with me right away. I kept saying, "But they're not on my list!"

My wife tried to be patient with me, but she didn't want to wait until January to get into MD Anderson. So, she made an appointment and dragged me to VCU to meet with Dr. Swainey.

As we walked into VCU, I couldn't help but remember another oncologist we'd met with a few weeks ago. He wasn't a warrior. He was passive. "There's really not much we can do, Mr. Callaghan. If you want to, you could maybe take a medicine—I mean, if you really want to—but we don't know if it would work, and it comes with a lot of side effects . . ."

Yes, I want to take the medicine! I want you to pull your sword out and fight for me! Needless to say, I walked out of there as fast as I could.

But Dr. Swainey? As soon as I met him, I knew he was the warrior for me. He not only looked into getting me into a trial that very first day but he also was able to get me to focus on my faith.

I always spent a good bit of time with my doctors telling them that it wasn't about me, it was about staying alive for Emma. Telling them how much I loved her. How much I would do anything, *anything,* to stay alive for her.

Dr. Swainey paused me mid sentence. "You know how much you love your daughter?" he said.

I gave him a look that said, *Haven't you been listening to me?*

He smiled at me and quietly said, "God loves her more."

Whew. Wow. Okay. Maybe I needed that.

He was officially my doctor.

Christmas was approaching. Another Christmas overshadowed

by cancer. Plus, this year the medical bills were really piling up. Paying the mortgage was a struggle. I had just sold some rare electronics and Star Wars collectibles just to make sure we covered the December mortgage payment. There wasn't much left for presents or special events.

The plan for your life far exceeds
the circumstances of today.
—Unknown

My mom doesn't know how to do subtle, though, and was generous enough to get my family a Chromecast. Okay, it was really a geeky present for me. I was thrilled and immediately went about setting it up. It was ready to go after lunch, and I called the family in so I could show them this new toy.

If you're not familiar with it, Google Chromecast allows phones and tablets to broadcast to your TV. So, I pulled out my phone and opened the YouTube app. The last video that I'd watched was still on my screen. It was a video of Alex titled "New Year's Resolution: 52 Weeks Later."

I hadn't yet talked to Lissa or Emma about the promise I'd made or told them anything about Alex. The promise had significantly affected me, but I didn't know how to bring it up without admitting that . . . I was preparing to die.

But I wanted them to be inspired too. It was Christmas and watching this video might be a nice way to focus on all the blessings surrounding us, despite the elephant in the room.

I queued up the video and explained how I had read about Alex and his mission. We sat and watched the short video, and Lissa and Emma seemed to enjoy it. Then we started to get ready for our annual Christmas walk with Noël.

The TV had been off for literally two minutes when my phone rang. I didn't recognize the number. Someone in Ohio? I didn't have any family there and wasn't going to talk to someone random on Christmas Day, so I didn't answer.

But then I felt this pull to figure out who it was. I didn't even wait to see if they left a voice mail message. I started Googling the number. After scrolling through several results, I saw this: "Because I Said I Would Founder Donates 20 Disneyland Trips to Children Diagnosed with Cancer."

What? Could it be that Alex? Had just called me? On Christmas?

Just seconds after I had introduced him and his mission to my family?

Sure enough, I had a voice mail message from him.

Hi, Garth. This is Alex Sheen, founder of Because I Said I Would. We messaged back in November but didn't have the opportunity to connect at that time. I just wanted to call and say "Happy Holidays" and get a chance to speak with you. Maybe another time. I hope you're having a great day and we'll talk soon. Have a great day.

Crazy.

I texted him back, thanking him for the call and telling him we'd connect soon.

My family and I headed off on our walk and my head felt like it was in the clouds. Obviously, I was touched that Alex would think to call me at all, let alone on Christmas Day. But I also just had this sense that something was happening. That there was a real reason why Alex and I were connecting in this way.

Lissa looked at me and my giddy smile. She put her mittened hand in mine. "This was clearly your best present."

And it really was.

Alex and I talked the next day. I'd forgotten that his whole mission had been inspired by his father's death from cancer. I cried. We cried together. Once again I was projected into a possible future with a fatherless Emma.

I hate when my mind goes to that future. It is difficult to pull out of that thought pattern.

Alex asked to write about my story on the Because I Said I Would Facebook page. I was more than happy to share. We spoke frequently over the next few weeks because Alex wanted to make sure that he was representing the facts correctly and that I was comfortable with the emotional side of the story as well. He kept asking if I was okay with him sharing my story. I thought, *Of course. If it helps a few people, I want to do it.* Alex cautioned me about how quickly my family could be thrust into the spotlight. I thought he was crazy. While sometimes videos went viral, it took a lot of time. And I didn't see anything viral about a sick dad who wrote some notes on napkins.

Learn to forgive.

Forgiveness is a gift that you give yourself. You don't need to forget. You just need to learn to let go and not allow that person or situation to control you.

I was laid off from Circuit City in early 2001. You were just a toddler, and Mom wasn't working. I had a fairly good severance package and was offered a job within two days of being laid off. In hindsight, it wasn't necessarily a rough situation. However, for years I held on to the bitterness of being laid off. I never shared my feelings of betrayal. I carried them silently. Those feelings poisoned many of my interactions with Circuit City for years to come. I was only harming myself. What made it worse was that I was angry at an institution, not a person!

We all need peace, and forgiveness allows us to let go of the hurt. Forgiveness is a decision, much like other decisions in your life. You can decide.

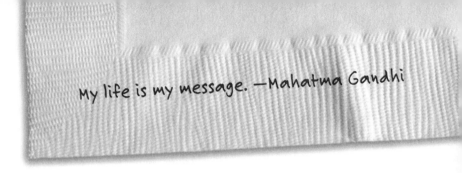

My life is my message. —Mahatma Gandhi

CHAPTER 16

Going Public

January 23, 2014

"What does high risk mean?" Garth asked. His oncologist looked him in the eyes and responded ... "You are going to die of this." Garth is forty-four years old and has been diagnosed with cancer three times since November 2011. Prostate cancer once. Kidney cancer twice. Although he appears healthy today, statistics say he has an 8 percent chance of living past five years.

Garth has one daughter named Emma. He has been writing napkin notes for Emma's lunch box since she was in the second

grade. They are just a few words of encouragement, but in the busy-
ness of their separate days at work and school, it's a moment when
they can connect. It's a moment when Garth knows she is thinking
about him.

Garth may die, but he will not let Emma eat lunch without that
note. This is his promise, to write one napkin note for every day of
class Emma has until she graduates from high school. To date, he
has completed 740 notes. 86 to go.

That was what Alex posted on his Facebook page. Two hours
after posting, I received an e-mail from Alex: "Your post on Facebook is pacing to be the most successful post we've ever had on
Facebook."

I'd been reading all the comments and was deeply moved by
the support I was receiving. I had shared the story on my Timeline
too. It had started to make the rounds from my circle of friends
and beyond.

Lissa came to me the next morning concerned. We hadn't
talked to Emma about the post. She wasn't on Facebook and neither were most of her friends. But this post obviously focused on
the grimness of my diagnosis more than we did. Lissa was worried

that Emma would have someone come up to her and essentially say, "I didn't know your dad was dying."

Ugh. Of course, that would be horrible. But my head was still stuck in the mud. "Lissa, Emma will never hear about this. It doesn't matter. No one is reading this story."

I sure got that one wrong.

As the story continued to spread, the next day I decided to talk to Emma. Emma knew I was a high-risk patient. We had never really defined what that meant except that I would be watched closely for new cancer and we were searching to find some treatment options that might help us keep the growth at bay.

I was driving Emma somewhere. I can't even remember why we were in the truck together. I took the opportunity to casually mention the story that was out there. I shared with her the statistics that were featured prominently.

Eight percent.

Five years.

I told her that I was a statistic of one. The numbers didn't apply to me. I believed that then and I still believe it. Our family would beat the odds. We weren't dry numbers on a spreadsheet.

I mentioned that she might not want to casually browse the

Internet and read stories about me. I shared that we might be asked to tell the story of cancer, but most important, we wanted to really talk about Napkin Notes and how much they meant to us. We wanted to help other parents connect better with their kids with Napkin Notes. This wasn't going to be about cancer. It most certainly wasn't going to be about dying. That would happen. We're all mortal. We can't avoid it.

Emma seemed to understand. I asked her if she had any concerns about telling the story. She shook her head. She was excited to be able to help.

LESSON #56:

Give your friend your last dollar.

Money is a thing. You can earn more. If you have a friend in need and you can afford it, give him the money. Heck, maybe you should give him the money even if you can't afford it. Don't ever loan a friend money. Don't ever loan your family money. Give them the money. If you loan the money, it will have strings even though you don't mean it to. At the very least, the recipient will see strings even though they might not be there.

> Know the difference between success and fame. Success is Mother Teresa. Fame is Madonna. —Erma Bombeck

CHAPTER 17

I'm Just a Guy Writing Napkins

It was a Tuesday morning and I was sitting at my desk at work when I received an odd text from my business coach, René Haines. "You were just on the *Today* show. Congratulations!"

I looked around. I was pretty sure I was at work, in my cubicle. I wasn't in New York City. I didn't know what she was talking about.

Alex had called just a few days after his Facebook post went crazy to ask me whether he could post my story on a few other sites, Reddit and Imgur. I'd agreed. He let me know to expect some calls for interviews. I chuckled. And then fielded a call from someone from Today.com. Eun Kim wanted to interview me for their website. I was taken aback but of course agreed. That call had been followed by hundreds of requests. BuzzFeed, Huffington Post, Yahoo. But all of this was online. I hadn't been on TV.

Somehow the "Today's Take" segment at the top of the nine o'clock hour had a story about me. They'd taken the content from the website interview and just discussed it live on air.

My cell phone started ringing off the hook. Nonstop. Napkin Notes had officially gone viral.

The next few days were a whirlwind of activity. Fielding requests. Having discussions as a family as to how far we were going to take this. Was I okay taking my daughter on air to discuss this very private, heartbreaking situation? But every time we talked, Emma was confident she could handle it. She loved the mission of Napkin Notes and was proud of everything that was happening. She wanted us to spread the message as far as it would go.

I was so impressed with my little girl.

I, however, felt conflicted the more I was thrust into the limelight. Every interviewer would praise me for what I was doing, tell me what a good father I was. I was grateful for their words, but really? I was writing notes on napkins. Yes, it was important.

Yes, somehow we needed to have these reminders of the simple things in our crazy, out-of-whack-priorities society. But these people weren't there on the days when the side effects of my medicine were unbearable and I had no patience left. When I snapped at Emma for taking too long getting ready for her softball practice and I was worried we would be late.

The point of Napkin Notes wasn't me, or even that I was dying. It was that everyone could be a Napkin Note dad. Everyone could take five minutes every day to do something special for the people they love. Pack their lunch. Write a note. Connect.

That's what was important. I was not.

Courage is being scared to death but saddling up anyway. —John Wayne

---

I was feeling overwhelmed as we prepared for our first trip to New York City. The *Today* show actually wanted us on air. I couldn't sleep. I couldn't think correctly. I wasn't able to process the tsunami of interest in our family.

On our first night in New York City, we stopped at St. Patrick's

Cathedral. Lissa wanted to look around, and I had never been there either. I felt this pressure in my chest and head as we walked in. Emma and I were just hours away from going on national TV to share our story. We would potentially be speaking to millions of parents and we hoped our mission would resonate, even if just a little. I said a tongue-in-cheek prayer at the back of the church—"Shepard's Prayer," rumored to have been uttered by astronaut Alan Shepard. I said it out loud so Lissa and Emma could hear.

"Dear Lord, don't let me f*** up."

I think Lissa and Emma were fully shocked. I generally don't cuss, and I certainly have never said anything like this in a church! It injected some levity into the situation but completely encompassed the weight I felt. What was I doing? I certainly hadn't planned on this sudden attention. What if I screwed up? What if I couldn't hold it together as I tried to share the feelings about my mortality and why Napkin Notes was so important to me?

Just a few hours earlier, when I had recorded a segment for NPR's *Here and Now,* I was completely unprepared to be asked, "Garth, first and foremost, everyone hearing this, including me, as I am having this conversation with you, hopes more than anything that when Emma receives napkin 826 that you are still here. In the event that that doesn't happen, what would you hope that she thinks about who you are when she gets to napkin 826 and looks back on this collection?" Holy frak! I couldn't believe she had just asked me this question while both Lissa and Emma were in the studio behind me, listening!

I choked. I literally choked on my own words and then sobbed. I felt like I had been stabbed in the heart. I couldn't hold it together, and thank goodness my back was to my family. I had been so used to telling this story in a positive light. Yes, I had had my fears and trials, but I had been able to work through most of that. I believed that a positive attitude was the best weapon in my arsenal. And with one question, my fears and doubts were not only on the battlefield but charging at me with full force.

Thank goodness NPR edited most of the sobbing and stuttering out. It didn't matter to me. I knew how I had felt and what had happened. I couldn't imagine doing that on national television. There was nowhere to hide with a television camera.

The next morning came, with the ridiculously early call time and a blessedly sensitive interviewer. Emma was amazing and I was able to hold it together. It was a surreal moment, one I still haven't watched. An experience I never would have expected

I'd have, especially with my little girl. (Who are we kidding? She looked like a young lady these days. So poised. So confident. And I was so proud.) This mission had taken on a new meaning. Cancer was quite a high price to pay to be able to share Napkin Notes. I thought, *God, is this what you're asking me to do? Really? I think I'd rather not have to deal with cancer and keep Napkin Notes between Emma and me. Okay?*

As I continued to be pushed up onto a pedestal, I struggled under the pressure. When it got to be too much, I picked up the phone and called my godmother, Aunt Ruth. She had always been my sanctuary. I'd often spent weekends with her and my uncle, Peter, when I'd lived close by. I'd given their sons fun gifts like fake dog poop and vomit when they were young. She and I had spent hours making a Super Mario castle cake for Jonathan's fifth birthday party. I was able to mentally decompress with them. I'd always felt safe there.

She listened to me talk for quite a while. Then she said exactly what I needed to hear. "Garth, you are not in this alone. You never have been. You don't need to worry about what to say. You've said it all. There are just more people who haven't heard. Pack. Write. Connect. This is less about cancer than about how much your girl

Whatever you are, be a good one.
—Abraham Lincoln

means to you, and a wonderful reminder to us all to take advantage of every small opportunity we have to tell those we love that they are *awesome!*"

Pack. Write. Connect.

I could do that. I follow that same advice today.

When I don't know what to do, or when I am consumed in the chaos of my life, I know what's most important.

Take a breath.

Pack a lunch.

Write a note.

Connect with Emma.

Repeat.

Nothing else matters.

You are a leader. Lead.

Emma, you are a leader. You have the skills to bring friends and teams together. Being a leader is not dependent upon a title. You can lead from within.

I see you. I know your frustrations when things aren't going right. You need to recognize that your team is looking to you. They will mimic your behavior. They will do what you suggest. If you let the situation dictate your mood, the team will pick up on that and follow you.

As you lead, delegate. You can't do everything on your own. Your actions and attitude will inspire the team.

One time, when I was a store manager at Circuit City Express, I stopped in at the store on my day off to see how things were going. I was wearing shorts and a T-shirt. I clearly wasn't dressed for work! I was chatting with one of the store associates and a customer walked right up to me and started asking questions about something. I answered quickly and politely. The customer was satisfied. I then asked the customer why he'd asked me, especially since I wasn't dressed as if I was working there. He replied that I clearly looked as if I was in charge, regardless of my dress.

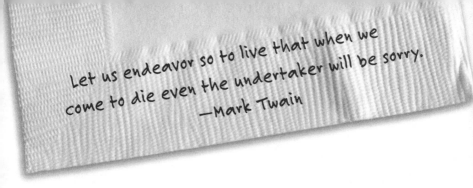

Let us endeavor so to live that when we come to die even the undertaker will be sorry.
—Mark Twain

CHAPTER 18

The Gift of Words

I paused before I folded the napkin. I was really hesitant to put anything about death in Emma's Napkin Notes these days. I didn't want her to focus on my mortality. I wanted her to focus on life. On her life. On how to live the best life possible. But this quote said that. I liked it. I folded it up and put it into her lunch bag.

I was feeling excited today. Dr. Swainey had called with the news that I wasn't accepted into the drug trial because of my prostate cancer. (Wouldn't you think because I had two kinds of cancer that I should have been at the top of the list? But alas, I would have thrown off their results.) Bless his heart, Dr. Swainey had found a way to get me the medicine anyway *and* have my insurance cover some of it. (Without insurance it would have cost me twelve thousand dollars a month.) I was so thankful to be aggressively going after the cancer, to have found a doctor who was committed to doing everything he could to keep me alive.

I have often been asked about the impact cancer has had on my life. I can't begin to explain how many aspects of my life it has changed. It has attacked all the major pillars of my life. It has shaken me to my core, and at times, I have felt that I've almost lost myself. I can easily say that it's not just me who has cancer. It's my whole family. We've been on the battlefield for years and will likely never leave this battlefield until the very end of my life.

This might be difficult for you to read. It was difficult for me to say it to myself the first time.

I can't wish that I never had cancer. I am not glad to have had it. I certainly wish, hope, and pray that I don't have it tomorrow. But I can't wish that I never got it.

Cancer has put me on this road. Cancer has led me to focus on what's important. And if I'm able to help others do that as well, who am I to say that I shouldn't be dealing with this?

I'm thankful for another reason. It has given me a wake-up call.

Most obviously to take stock of my blessings, to tell those I care about that I love them. But also, to prepare. To get things in order. Life insurance. My will. What my wishes are about my funeral.

As I've mentioned before, my dad was the town undertaker in Port Leyden for thirty-four years. Death was a way of living for my family. I grew up knowing that death was a fact of life, something you wanted to avoid, for as long as possible, but if it happened, the Callaghan Funeral Home was there to support the family and try and make the transition as easy as possible.

Yet when my dad died a few months shy of my first cancer diagnosis, it was the first death I truly experienced. My grandparents had all passed away when I was younger, but that was a rite of passage. I had an uncle that passed away a few years before dad, but I wasn't super close to him. This was the first time one of my lifelines was gone. My dad was a rock, for me and many people around him. Losing him turned my world upside down.

Needless to say, I was surprised when Dad died. Although he didn't lead an incredibly healthy lifestyle, I don't think any of us expected him to die when he did. His doctor thought he might have lung cancer. There were some spots on his lung, and there was reason to believe it could be cancer. Dad was a lifelong smoker.

I think he started smoking in elementary school.

Dad had a biopsy to check it out. It went as well as most biopsies go, but he suffered a collapsed lung shortly after. He lapsed into a coma and never woke up.

I had driven up to visit my dad after he slipped into his coma. There wasn't much to do. There wasn't anything to say. We weren't sure whether he would pull out of it or not.

We had only been on the road home an hour when I got the call. Dad was gone. It was sudden from my perspective. I never got to say good-bye. I didn't even have the chance to talk to him because of the coma.

I was unprepared for the cascade of emotions I felt during that time. My first thought as we drove back to Port Leyden was, "Who buries the undertaker?" In many cases, it is the son, who has gone into the family business. I did not. I was a bystander at best, the son who chose not to follow in his father's footsteps. I was the son who moved away and saw his parents a couple of times each year. Neither my sister, Colleen, nor I went into the business, but she was at least physically closer to home. (On a side note, my mom, though she was sixty-nine when my dad died, decided to keep running the funeral home herself.)

We didn't really prepare for Dad's death. We should have. For crying out loud, the family business was death! I am unaware of any family conversations surrounding our parents, or what was expected of us after one died. I don't know if dad had any specific wishes. I know he often said that funerals and their details were for the family that was left. I didn't know what I wanted for him. We never talked about it.

Mom didn't even have a current will and had to dig up a forty-year-old document for managing the estate. (I think I was supposed to go live with my Uncle Harold and Aunt Gigi, but considering I was forty-two, everyone felt it was okay if I stayed on my own!)

Why did we avoid this discussion? Dying is part of life. Last I checked, we all have a 100 percent chance of dying. Our family's mission was to help the families of Port Leyden after the death of a loved one, yet we avoided the topic within our own household.

I don't know if I can even begin to describe growing up with my dad. I am sure everyone has similar stories about good times and bad times. There were times I felt extremely close to dad, and conversely, there were times I felt he was incredibly distant and uninvolved. I know my dad loved my sister, Colleen, and me very much. I think there were times he had difficulty expressing that love. When he did show his love and support, it was absolutely immense.

One thing I know for sure is that my dad helped to instill the value of hard work at an early age. I remember one time that I needed some money to pay for a class trip. Dad wasn't simply going to turn over the cash. I needed to "earn" it and on that day, he decided that I'd earn it by beating him at a game. We pulled out a massive cardboard box. I can't even imagine what was originally inside of this container, but the box could have easily been used as a playhouse for three or four kids. We folded in the flaps, and played "basketball" using the box as the hoop. Thank goodness! I was fairly young and not very good at regular basketball, but this box I could hit! My dad didn't let me win that afternoon. He didn't subscribe to the theory that you let your child win just because he's a child. Winning was earned.

Dad taught me to play chess when I was pretty young. He had a special chess set. The chess pieces were wonderfully smooth and shiny. The chessboard itself had seen better days. He and his best friend had played often when they were in college together. I learned one opening sequence, the Sicilian Defense, and used it all of the time. We played and played and played. I can't count how many times we played before I finally won. I don't even think I realized I had checkmated him.

We had marathon Monopoly games. The game would often start out as a family event with mom and Colleen, too. The game would quickly narrow down to Dad and me, and we could continue playing for hours. One of our games actually lasted days with the playing board being preserved overnight for the next day. Each battle, each win, was savored.

And then there was pinochle. Pinochle was a true family game. I know there are still score sheets lying around the house serving as permanent records of games played long ago. I am pretty sure all members of both sides of my family played pinochle, and I will never forget the moment when I was finally invited to sit at the table. I was honored not only because the family considered me mature enough to play, but if I played, that meant that one of the grown-ups had to sit out. My family showed infinite patience as I learned. Pinochle is a difficult card game and there are many nuances that influence gameplay. Everyone seemed to be three steps ahead of me and I had no idea how they were so good! I was partnered with my dad one game, and he had won the bid. I was so happy because I had a run in the suit he called, and I promptly laid it down . . . before I had passed him cards. I screwed up! We had to throw out the hand, and I have never forgotten that game. My dad was so disappointed, but carefully explained what I should do in the event that situation ever happened again. It didn't, but I never forgot that lesson.

Winning required learning.

I definitely earned the extras I needed in life. Mom and Dad believed that we should have new sneakers when we needed them, but if we wanted the "special" shoes or something better than the average ones we'd pick up at the local department store, Colleen and I were responsible for the price difference. When I wanted to join the downhill ski team, I paid for my equipment myself.

In order to earn this extra money, I worked for my dad. I think most sons who work for their dads would agree this is a difficult situation. Although I started my first job outside of the family at age eleven, delivering newspapers for the *Watertown Daily Times,* my primary job was "helper" at the Callaghan Funeral Home. When I was younger, I was in charge of mowing the lawn, washing the hearse, and shoveling the walks. In Northern New York, shoveling snow was a never-ending job for six months of the year! There were many times I would have to start over as soon as I had finished.

Whatever the job, my dad had an expectation that I would do the job right. If I left a "weenie row" of grass because I had carelessly steered incorrectly, I needed to go back over that section so the grass was evenly cut. It was better for me to fix my error than to have Dad ask me to fix it. I was expected to fix the mistakes if I made them, or else I wouldn't get paid.

Washing the hearse was my least favorite task. Hearses are tall. I couldn't easily reach the roof. The roof was black, and I had to dry it before water spots formed. The hubcaps had spokes, at least fifty per tire. I spent many hours cleaning those hubcaps with a toothbrush. Oh, how I hated that! Why couldn't our hearse have normal hubcaps? When I was finished with that part of the job, I had to move on to cleaning the whitewalls. It seemed as if washing the hearse was a job that went on and on, and I had to do that chore each time someone passed away.

As I grew up, my responsibilities grew, too. I was often in charge of arranging the flowers, moving and setting up chairs, and cleaning up the funeral home before calling hours. I even helped my dad remove bodies from homes and wheel caskets around. My dad saw to it that there was much care taken with each of these responsibilities.

It wasn't until I was much older that I realized some of the lessons that my dad was instilling in me. Frankly, I don't even know if he was trying to instill those lessons or if they were an unintended by-product.

1. Take pride in your work.
2. Do it right the first time.
3. Your work isn't always about you.

Although cleaning those spokes on the hearse was tedious, there was a fundamental reason behind the effort my dad required. It wasn't just having pride in your own work. It wasn't just doing a job right. It was because there was a fundamental respect that we, the Callaghans, wanted to show the family of the deceased. Port Leyden is a small town. We knew everyone. We knew the family of the deceased. We had to show respect to the deceased, the family, and even the town. We weren't just shoveling the snow to keep the walks clean. The act of shoveling snow was more about keeping the walks clear so that family members could safely make it into the funeral home. It was so they didn't slip or struggle up the sidewalk. The family and friends were struggling enough with the death of their loved one. They didn't need to have trouble walking up to the funeral home, and it was my job to make that walk as easy as possible for them.

Act as if what you do makes
a difference. It does.
—William James

I was diagnosed with cancer just a few months after my dad's death. I didn't really get a chance to fully grieve my dad because now I needed to grieve for myself. My feelings about my dad's death were overshadowed by my fears for my own.

It is only recently that I realized how deeply I miss my dad. I was in the middle of a radio interview about Napkin Notes when somehow my dad came to mind. "I am a mission-driven father, and my mission is to get to every parent, to inspire them to write to their kids. Whether it's once a day or once a week, that these parents will make the commitment and write a short note to them. My dad passed away a couple of years ago and . . . there's nothing I wouldn't give to have a note or a letter from my dad. At this point, it's too late."

There's nothing I wouldn't give to have a note or a letter from my dad. At this point, it's too late.

I was choked up with emotion suddenly and had to take a few deep breaths to keep talking. This deep sadness overwhelmed me and I realized that, at that moment, I wasn't thinking about Emma losing her dad, I was just thinking about how much it hurt to lose mine.

Mom heard my interview. She knew that there must be something in the house that might qualify as a note from dad. She scoured the house. She dug through boxes of old report cards, crayon pictures, crafts, and award certificates in search of a letter or a note.

She found one. Although she kept the original, she scanned it and mailed both Colleen and me a copy. I knew what it was as soon as I opened the envelope. I recognized my dad's handwriting immediately. I put the letter back into the envelope and burst into sobs. Despite the fact it was exactly what I had been craving, I wasn't ready to read it. It was just after I'd been diagnosed for the fourth time and I didn't want to read a letter from my deceased father. It was too much.

I finally pulled the letter out a few months later. It came from a letter-writing exercise that my parents went through as part of a Marriage Encounter weekend in 1978.

11/15

Dear Family,

Most of the time I feel very proud of the job that Garth and Colleen do in school.

Dad was a lazy student and now I'm ashamed and embarrassed by the marks I got in grade school—if you ever saw my old report cards you'd give me an A-T-T-I-T-U-D-E spanking.

When Mommy and I go for conferences or even when we just run into your teachers, they almost always say terrific things about both of you and about your work—it gives me warm fuzzies about our children.

Sometimes I feel disappointed that you don't work harder on the things you don't like—if you don't like it, it's usually the subject you put off doing till last—and it's also the one you need to do the most. You're not kidding me at all—if you don't like it, it's only because it's hard.

God was very good to Mom and I—he gave us 2 children that are very smart—usually you don't even need to study to get good marks and when you put effort into your work it's usually 100% papers.

Garth—Sometimes Garth has a problem because when "you're #1— why try harder?" Well, "Try harder and you'll always be #1."

Colleen—I know Colleen got a bad start this year and wasn't doing her work but then new Colleen is doing a good job. Mrs. O'Connor can't be fooled and she wouldn't lie to me.

To sum it all up I feel very lucky to have two kids that do such a good job.

Amen,

Dad

That's it. Those are the only written words I have from my dad. There may be more, but this is what I have today.

It's not much but I'm thankful that I have it. A reminder of Dad's concern and care. He knew me well. I was always pretty gifted in school, but if it wasn't something I was interested in, I tended to ignore those lessons. I struggled with fractions. I had struggled with multiplication tables the year before. (I love math now, thank goodness!) I remember one dinner when fractions and math got the best of me. Mom was traveling to Saranac Lake during the week. Papa (Grandpa Keough) was battling cancer and it wasn't going well. Mom was a nurse and would spend the week up there. She'd make dinners all weekend and freeze them. We were going to have pea soup one day, and dad decided it should be my job to make the cornbread. I grabbed a box of Jiffy Corn Muffin Mix from the pantry and started getting the recipe together. It called for "⅓ cup of milk." I didn't know fractions. I read this as one three-cup measurement of milk and added three cups of milk. Gosh, it was soupy. I had no idea what I did wrong and finally asked Dad for help.

It probably doesn't need to be said that Dad was frugal. He grew up in a family that didn't have much to waste, and throwing away a box of Jiffy Cornbread was out of the question. His solution? Add more boxes of cornbread until it evened out. We were eating cornbread for weeks!

I'm not sure that memory would have resurfaced except for reading that letter.

We live in a digital age. I'm a techy guy and love to use my tablet and my cell phone to text and e-mail. But there is something about a written letter that lasts. Do you ever go back into your e-mails to reread things? Probably not. But if you're sorting through a certain drawer, and come upon a handwritten note, odds are you'll stop and read it. You'll pause and reconnect with the writer, be reminded of something you've long forgotten, feel emotional at the sight of handwriting that is so unique to each individual.

Don't wait. The time will never be just right.
—Napoleon Hill

I can't even begin to count how many Napkin Notes I have written. Even if I could estimate how many Emma has received, I started mailing out notes to friends last year. Then I started mailing notes to people I didn't even know, people who needed a pick-me-up. There were some cancer warriors I could tell needed to receive notes. I would often surreptitiously find out their addresses, write a handful of notes, and mail them out. I would usually "forget" to write a return address on the envelope. I really enjoyed the knowledge that I'd make someone's day and they'd have no idea how it had happened.

I have received a handful of Napkin Notes too. Each one is treasured. God seemed to know when I might need to receive a note and provided it at just the right time.

My first note came shortly after my third diagnosis. It was a particularly difficult time for me. It started with a scheduling conflict with my CT scan and prostate biopsy. I was hoping to have both in the same day, but because I had some lovely contrast in my stomach, I couldn't have the sedative before my prostate biopsy. I wasn't willing to wait. But I remembered all too well the pain of my first prostate biopsy and how I'd vowed I would never do it without a sedative again. It was frustrating, but I was bound and determined to undergo the biopsy regardless of how much pain it might cause.

Nurse Kaky Minter has always been the assistant for the prostate biopsy procedures. She's a warm and caring nurse. She has genuine concern for her patients, and she knew I was submitting to the biopsy without my desired sedative.

The procedure was completed somewhat quickly, and I wiped away a couple of tears. She also knew that I had just had a CT scan and therefore hadn't eaten since the day before. Nurse Kaky made sure I had some crackers and ginger ale to help right my systems again. We chatted about Napkin Notes as I was eating the crackers. She had seen the newspaper article. It was a nice diversion from the literal pain in my butt.

I was diagnosed with kidney cancer a day later and started making plans for a new battle.

From Nurse Kaky—November 17, 2013

It arrived in a regular envelope. I had no idea what was inside. I could tell it wasn't another medical bill, and for that I was thankful. But when I opened the envelope, I was beside myself. Someone sent *me* a Napkin Note. Up until that very moment, I had only written Napkin Notes for others, mostly Emma. I had never really thought about how receiving a Napkin Note would change me.

Hey Mr. Callaghan,

Thought you should receive a napkin note. I wanted to let you know how much I enjoyed meeting you and what an inspiration your story is. I ran across the article in the paper again the other day and have shared it with many.

Thank you for your story and the lives you are touching.
Keep up the good work!

Sincerely,

Kaky Minter

At the very end, she'd added:

Triumph—umph added to try

I felt tears bubble to the surface again. Man, this cancer certainly was making me a crybaby. I shook my head in disbelief. I had needed to read her closing more than anything. Fighting cancer is a long battle. It requires a lot of focus and energy. There are days when I am running only on reserves and hide it so my family doesn't worry. This Napkin Note filled up my mental and spiritual reserves and kept them full for weeks.

Emma's First Napkin Note—January 13, 2014

I have been writing Napkin Notes to my daughter, Emma, for years. January 13, 2014, marked the first time my daughter wrote a

Napkin Note for me and secretly put it into my lunch box.

I walked into work that morning exactly as I did any other business day. I carried both my breakfast and my lunch. I chatted with my coworkers as I opened the lunch box to pull out my oatmeal. I saw a paper towel next to my food. I looked at the paper towel and thought it was odd. I was sure I hadn't put anything like that in there. It took me a minute to realize that someone else had probably placed it in my lunch box.

I smiled in anticipation.

I opened the paper towel and saw a note:

If my friends really did jump off a cliff, it's because it was my idea.
Sincerely, your daughter is a leader, not a follower.
P.S. I think you used all the napkins <3

Emma had put a Napkin Note in my lunch. She had even sneaked it in there without my knowledge! My eyes welled up. I took the note, walked around the office, and showed everyone I could find. My daughter had written a note to *me*! I had been giving her notes for years. I knew she loved them, but this was proof that they really meant something to her!

When I got home from work that day, I gave her a big hug and asked her what had inspired her.

She breathed deeply. "Dad, I don't do enough for you. You do everything for me. And I had just found a really good saying to write on the note!"

Emma's Second Napkin Note—January 15, 2014

It happened again.

Emma snuck a Napkin Note into my gear before I left for work. The joy I felt was utterly incredible. I had started something, and Emma was picking it up and giving back. This was awesome! My daughter, to whom I have been writing Napkin Notes for years, was now communicating to me in the same way.

The new note read:

An arrow can only be shot by pulling it backward. So, when life is dragging you back, it means it's going to launch you into something awesome!

Life had been dragging me back, even though I had been resisting with all my might. It had been a long winter and I was tired. I was battle weary. The battle was taking a toll on a lot of fronts.

That day we had a big win. Our heat pump was ancient. It was well past its serviceable years. I had been wondering all winter long if it would finally give up its ghost. That afternoon I received a call from James River Air Conditioning and they were giving us a substantial discount on a new system! We could look forward to a cool summer!

That day I was the arrow.

Terry Martin—March 7, 2014

Lent had started. I was stopping in at church to chat with Ed Golden, the Grand Knight of St. Michael's Knights of Columbus. I had sought out the Knights of Columbus at my church back when I was struggling in my faith. The Knights of Columbus was formed in 1882 by Father Michael J. McGivney in part to help Catholic families whose breadwinner had died. I was very concerned about leaving my family with a mountain of medical bills. The Knights also had a program in which I could receive some assistance with those very same medical bills.

That group of men became so much more than I had imagined.

I joined after a few months. Each meeting started with prayers, and the entire group was praying for me and success with my battle. The knights welcomed me with open arms. I felt safe with them. Cared for.

I hadn't planned on staying for the Friday fish fry. Besides, Lissa was making dinner. As I was chatting with Ed, one of my fellow knights came over and asked if we were coming to the fish fry. I explained that we had other plans, but he didn't want to hear it. They were going to make a to-go bag for my family.

It was incredibly kind. I was thankful. The to-go bag represented a caring group of men. It meant Lissa didn't have to make dinner. It was a lifeline of nourishment and goodwill.

I arrived home, excited to share the goodie bag with my family. We all filled our plates and sat down for a movie night. Emma was the last to load up her plate, and she found a Napkin Note in the bag.

Garth,

You are touching lives in such a positive way. . . .
You are an inspiration and I admire you greatly.

Terry

Terry Martin, the man who had brought me into the Knights of Columbus, had written a Napkin Note to me. Once again, I was floored. I needed that message exactly when I received it.

I am amazed at how each of these notes reached me at the precise moment when I needed a lift. Needed a reminder that what I was doing mattered. That there were moments of victory even when I felt mired in defeat.

Words are powerful tools. They can tear down and they can build up. Every day we hold that power.

Build a team better than you.

I was incredibly fortunate to have the teams I have worked with. I can honestly say that all of my teams far superseded my abilities. My teams at Circuit City Express were able to take direction and completely run with it. They were able to achieve goals even when I wasn't there to lead. They were independent and great trouble-shooters. I trusted them to get the job done.

When I was with the company 127TECH, I learned to provide direction at the beginning of a project and let the project run. I would, when possible, provide guidance. We were often broken up into smaller groups and not able to communicate with one another. We needed to trust that each of us was completing the tasks at hand. Not only did I hire strong associates but I also hired people who filled gaps and were able to make up for my shortcomings.

Build your life team to be better than you alone. Build your family. Build your work team. Support them as a leader and let them support you as your team.

Round Four

You know all those things you wanted to do?
Go and do them.
Love, Dad

Until God opens the next door, praise him in the hallway. —Unknown

CHAPTER 19

Side Effects

I
t was February, just ten days after I'd officially started taking the new medicine that was supposed keep my kidney cancer at bay. It was time for my six-month scan. Yep. You may have guessed it. I had more cancer. Kidney again. Three to five lesions on my kidney. And something else on my remaining adrenal gland.

Luckily, I was already on the drug that they would have put me on anyway. Dr. Swainey had made it clear: "This drug is the best and last opportunity we have. If it doesn't work, we have to scramble. Obviously, we have plan B and C and D, probably all the way up to K. But we really hope this drug works."

It's medicine that truly makes me feel horrible. Like death. But if it keeps me around, you know I'm going to try it.

I have some good days and I have some bad days. Overall, I don't feel fantastic. The drugs frankly kick my butt. I knew it wasn't going to be an easy ride. The side effects are somewhat problematic:

- *diarrhea (Check! Double check!! Triple check!!!)*

- *fatigue (Check!)*

- *nausea (Check!)*

- *change in hair color (Check!)*

- *loss of taste (Check! Most things taste like they're black and white, but I want to eat in an HD world!)*

- *loss of appetite (Check! I have lost about twenty pounds.)*

- *vomiting (Just once, but holy crap, it was awful.)*

- *pain on the right side of the abdominal area (Check!)*

- *easy bruising (Check!)*

- *irregular or rapid heartbeat (Check!)*

- *fainting (Not yet, thankfully.)*

- *bleeding problems (Check! How I love the indignity of a bloody nose.)*

- *high blood pressure (Check!)*
- *thyroid problems (Check!)*

Let me be clear. I am thankful—yes, thankful—to be taking this medicine. It represents the best possible chance for me to beat cancer. It certainly comes with some challenges. I'll take them each and every day.

Someone asked me if this was chemo. It's not. Technically, it's not anywhere close to chemo. However, it's easy to say that it's "like chemo," except that I take this every day and I don't really get a break. I don't experience all the side effects at the same time, but I certainly am plagued with some of the tougher ones.

I have to have my blood checked every other week because one of the side effects of this medicine is liver failure. The other day Lissa and I were at my doctor's office. He'd taken me off the medicine for a few days because my liver wasn't handling it well. He was also concerned about the cumulative impact of the side effects. I was in rough shape and not dealing with the medicine very well either.

I rebutted his desire to have me take a break. "I am a full-dose patient. I want to go on the record that I don't like this."

He smirked a little and replied, "So noted."

I wasn't going to win this battle, especially not with Lissa in the room. She was a witness.

Lissa knew that my body was stressed and I was close to reaching my physical limits. She asked the doctor, "How long will he be taking this?"

The doctor turned to face my wife. And he said, "For-ev-er." Like that. Spaced out. As if the word "forever" wasn't dramatic enough.

I will most likely take this medicine for the rest of my life. Think about that for a second before you move on.

I may take this for the rest of my life. What would you do? You'd take the darned medicine. Give your body a chance to win! Live! Raise your kids! Change the world!

What would you do to live?

This. This is what I do. Medically, it's what I'll likely do for the rest of my life.

Every night, before I go to bed, I walk into my bathroom. I take the pill bottle down from its shelf in my bathroom cabinet. I pour the tablets into the palm of my hand. I close my eyes and pray: "Dear God, please let this medicine kill my cancer." On some days, I'll add the caveat "And please, if possible, let's minimize the side effects." Most of the time I don't add that prayer. I know what's really important.

And through this chaos of medicine and side effects, I'll take a breath. I'll pack Emma's lunch. I'll write a Napkin Note. I'll connect with her one more time.

Pack. Write. Connect. Repeat.

It's okay to have a job that's a little bit lower than your skills.

One of the very best assistant managers worked with me at the Circuit City Express in Copley Place. Alan Ware was simply a phenomenal person and a great assistant manager. I know he was offered many promotions to become a store manager. He was happy working as an assistant manager and didn't want the added responsibility (read: hassle!) that came along with being a store manager. He wanted time to cultivate his passion for music—he was a fantastic drummer.

I greatly respect Alan's decision to turn down promotions. He knew what he wanted from his job and was completely satisfied being an assistant manager even though he was more than qualified to be more.

As you grow older you will discover that you have two hands. One for helping yourself, the other for helping others. —Audrey Hepburn

CHAPTER 20

Lifelines

eing alone with your thoughts can be a dangerous place, especially for a cancer patient.

When I was first diagnosed with cancer, I was by myself. I heard the dreaded words "You have cancer" and the rest of the appointment slowed to a crawl. Although there were plenty of things said, explanations given and initial plans laid out, I couldn't hear. I was truly alone. There was no one to steady me. There was no one to hear what the doctor was saying. There was no one to hold my hand. I left his office and walked out of the building. I got back into my car and drove home.

Alone. Lissa and Emma weren't there. I was still alone.

I was alone for about three hours that afternoon. I haven't been alone since.

My entire family has cancer. The cancerous cells are only in my body, but cancer is impacting us far and wide. Lissa, Emma, my mother, and my sister have all felt the wretched impact of this disease. We all feel sick. We are equally worried. We go to the doctor appointments together. We wait for results together. Now that I am taking medicine, we have bad days together. When there are good MRI results, we celebrate together.

I am surrounded by caregivers. Without them, I don't know where I'd be.

Lifeline #1: Emma

When I was first diagnosed, I thought Emma was handling it well. The initial conversation was tough and there were fears expressed and some tears. I had to make sure she understood what cancer meant from a practical standpoint in addition to including a medical explanation. She seemed to be a fairly normal Emma after that.

There weren't worried looks, and I didn't see much concern on her face.

I didn't know that she and Lissa were actively hiding Emma's concerns from me. There was no malice intended. I had to wait about six weeks until my first surgery. They knew that I was stressed and had plenty of my own fears, and they were sheltering me.

Emma and Lissa would snuggle at bedtime. I would often poke my head into Emma's room and give Emma a kiss goodnight, but I didn't want to interrupt their time together. I later learned that time was spent talking about me, cancer, surgery, and the various concerns surrounding what was happening in our family.

I know that Emma has sacrificed due to my battle. I haven't had the energy level she was used to. I have missed opportunities to play with her. She hasn't received a regular allowance in over two years. We signed her up late for softball in 2014 and she didn't make it past the waiting list. (That worked out in the end because we joined a neighboring team and that team is *fantastic*! Go Rockville!)

Lately, she accepts my battle and is helping in the fight. Her worst days are the days when I feel unwell. She doesn't like it when I am suffering and she feels somewhat helpless. She looks out for me. She's always there to cover me with a blanket, get me a drink, or forgo a nighttime tuck-in without complaint. It's humbling to miss an opportunity to tuck her in because I am too tired and already in bed. On those nights, she tucks me in and gives me a kiss goodnight. For fourteen years I tucked her in. She now tucks me in. I am not ready to have my daughter take care of me, but we all have made adjustments during this illness.

Emma has also graciously allowed me to tell our story and has joined me in that endeavor. I cannot even express what it is like to watch my fourteen-year-old daughter not only appear on national television with poise and grace but answer gut-wrenching questions about what she'll do without me with a calmness that astonishes me. She has become someone I look up to, admire, and am in awe of.

Lifeline #2: Colleen

My sister, Colleen, and I were never very close growing up. I couldn't say why. We're close in age, just two and a half years apart, but I was a very difficult act to follow. Our parents often tried to force us to play together by giving us complementary toys. I'd receive a *Six Million Dollar Man* doll and Colleen would receive the mission control center made for Steve Austin. These tactics would often end in disastrous results, tears, and some bruises.

Once, while we were painting my bedroom walls a different color, I walked up behind her and ran the handle of my paintbrush down her back. Of course, I had some paint dripping from the bristles so it appeared as if I had painted her back. She whipped around and grazed my chest with a dab of paint. I pretended to freak out and told her I had only faked painting her back. I yelled, "I am telling Mom!" and she immediately dunked her paintbrush and proceeded to paint her shirt up and down while pleading, "Please don't tell. Please don't tell."

I am happy to say my relationship with Colleen matured and strengthened as we grew older. It is a rare day when one of us isn't texting the other. We're always sharing pictures of our kids with each other. I genuinely enjoy being her brother. I rely on her for mental support. She's always there to boost me up. I wish that we lived closer to each other than we do. We only get to see each other about once a year, and that's not enough.

I know my battle has gravely injured her. I don't even know the extent of her pain. She has always been emotional when we've said good-bye and parted ways after a visit, but since I have had cancer, those good-byes are more poignant and tearful. She is my number-one Star Wars shirt supporter. I can't even count how many cards and letters I have received from her. I know Colleen and her husband, Rob, would do anything within their power to heal and support me.

Lifeline #3: Mom

I am sure that it is difficult for a mother to watch her child battle cancer at any age. I tried to protect my mom at times. I didn't want her to face an undue burden as we went through this battle, especially on the heels of losing my dad. She has faced this battle as if I were still her little boy, living at home and in fourth grade.

Unfortunately, she has had to mostly watch from the sidelines. There is little she can actively do. She tries to lift me up on days when I struggle, and she is there to join in when things are going well.

Mom still lives in my hometown of Port Leyden, New York. It's a close-knit community. It has to be. There are only about six hundred residents. In 2013, shortly after my third diagnosis, she mentioned that she wanted to hold a benefit for me. I wasn't sure what that entailed, but she explained that all I needed to do was to show up if I was healthy enough.

I was hesitant about asking for financial help in this manner. Port Leyden is not a well-off community. How could I ask these people for assistance? I had continued to hope that something would just make the stack of medical bills go away. That didn't happen. It wasn't going to happen. My doctors were convinced that I was going to be battling cancer somehow, in some way, for the rest of my life.

But I knew my mom was anxious to put her nervous energy to use. I had no idea if she had ever pulled together anything like this before. I chatted with Mom and let her know that I was open to a benefit and that I would do my best to make it back to Port Leyden for the event.

She and Colleen began planning. To this day, I still don't know everything that needed to be done to pull this off. They planned for about three months. There was a committee of about a dozen people—old high school friends, neighbors, and church members. Every once in a while Mom would ask for my opinion about some-

thing regarding the benefit. At one point, after I had just started taking the adjuvant therapy medicine and was combating various side
effects, I asked to be uninvolved. I could wait and be surprised as I
arrived in Port Leyden. I trusted them to handle everything well.

I flew home to Port Leyden the evening before the benefit. It
was a long flight that morphed into a ninety-minute drive from
the airport to a local hotel. (The Edge Hotel. Stay there! The owner,
Tracy Hurilla, and her staff make this the best place to stay in all
of Northern New York. It's Emma's favorite hotel. She even wrote
an essay about it.)

I woke up early on Saturday, too early. I had some breakfast in
the lobby and took advantage of the quiet time to write. It was still
dark outside, my favorite time of morning. Sadly, it was just too
early for someone battling cancer and I had to go back to bed after
a couple of hours. Mom popped over to the hotel for a visit before
the benefit got underway, but I was asleep. I can't imagine how she
felt knowing I was literally feet away from her but so fast asleep I
didn't even hear her knocking on the door.

After I woke up again and ate a second breakfast, I got ready
to drive the few miles back to Port Leyden. It was surreal arriv-
ing at the Fire Hall, a hallmark of my childhood. This served as a

community center for our small town. It's where the public pool is, where Little League games are held, and the location of many major events. The sign outside stated, "Garth Callaghan Benefit April 26." April 26 is also my mom's birthday. I was sure she had planned to have the benefit on that date so I would be home for her!

I walked into the Fire Hall and immediately saw Colleen. We hugged and chatted for a bit. I was impressed and overwhelmed at the amount of items donated for the auction. There were hundreds of items donated and more food than could possibly be eaten. There was everything from a homemade stool with a Star Wars quote etched into the top to a bookshelf shaped like a canoe. There were wine gift baskets, a Canadian-themed gift basket, and a cookbook with an autographed photo from Rachael Ray. Seriously? My mom had reached out to Rachael Ray to submit something for the auction? I couldn't imagine my mom doing that, let alone Rachael offering something.

I walked around for just a minute before my mom saw me. She practically tripped over herself as she quickly crossed the crowded room to get to my side. This was the first time Colleen and Mom had seen me with my new white hair, a side effect of the medicine I was taking. She hugged me tightly and clearly didn't want to let me go. It was a bittersweet reunion. I was glad to be there but humbled by the reason.

As I scanned the hall, my eyes fell on a quilt that was hanging up at the end of the room. I approached, knowing what it was but still not believing my eyes. It was a quilt containing a hundred napkin-size squares, and in each of the squares was stitched a Napkin Note quote. This was the first time I had seen such a tribute to the Napkin Notes movement. My eyes welled up with tears. It was beautiful, and I couldn't imagine the effort required to create this masterpiece.

The next seven hours were somewhat of a blur. It was a long day. Hundreds of people attended. There were classmates from high school; friends from Port Leyden, church, and nearby towns; former teachers; and even family friends who had traveled from Canada! I chatted with friends I hadn't seen in years. I met new friends. Close relatives drove from around the state to visit. The auction lasted hours. I needed to sit down. I needed to eat. I did neither. Aunt Ruth tried to make me do both, but she couldn't keep her eyes on me all the time.

We finally started to clean up a little after six. I was wiped out and feeling both tired and nauseated.

As the cleanup wrapped up, I said good-byes and thanked everyone who had helped out. I made my way back to The Edge and contemplated the gravity of the day. All the people who had attended; volunteered; donated time, talent, and treasure . . . they had done it all to help me and my family. I cried. I was moved beyond words. And for the first time in years, I was looking forward to paying my medical bills.

Would you believe that the auction my mom pulled together raised enough money to cover about 75 percent of my medical bills? I still can't believe it. And I'm grateful beyond words.

Lifeline #4: Lissa

Of course, my primary caregiver has been Lissa. She has made so many adjustments to accommodate my battle. I know there are times she is stressed beyond belief. I don't know how she can manage this every day.

Lissa has kept our family going. She has readjusted to a new normal time and again. She has kept our daughter's spirits up. She has kept my spirits up. She picks up my slack when I am out of physical or mental energy. I haven't mowed the lawn for at least a

Dear Emma, Make sure your friends know how important they are to you. Love, Dad year. That was always my given chore in our marriage. Lissa just quietly started doing the task herself. I'm beyond grateful that I didn't have to admit to her it was something I just couldn't do anymore.

Lissa sat in the room with me as Dr. Swainey told me that I would die from kidney cancer. She heard those words at the same moment I did. I couldn't breathe for a second. This was the first time Lissa had heard these words so directly stated. She also interpreted Dr. Swainey's words to mean "Let's look at this differently now. Let's find another way." I hadn't heard that. Thank goodness she was there.

We've found a new normal, again. Lissa is really watching out for me and my best interests. She knows the side effects from my treatment and is attuned to each one. The other day I was sitting in the dugout at one of Emma's softball games. The bleachers were in the sun, and there was just no way I was going to make it there. I didn't like being the only parent sitting in the hubbub of the dugout, but I didn't want to miss watching Emma play. So, there I sat, in the dark dugout. All of a sudden, I started to feel light-headed. It hit me out of nowhere. Before I knew it, Lissa was by my side with a handful of grapes and a bottle of water. I don't know how she got there so quickly from her spot on the bleachers, let alone how she could sense that I wasn't doing well. Thank goodness she did!

She's always there for me. I feel incredibly sad that I have brought this burden to her. She deserves better. Yet she doesn't think that. She knows she signed up for life with me when we were married that day in the funeral home. For better and for worse. I'm hoping we get lots more betters in the years ahead.

My life would be completely awful if I had to face this on my own, without family to lift me up. I'm beyond fortunate that through all of this I have had four rocks beneath me, steadying me, holding me up, supporting me. I am forever grateful.

These are the things that matter. If this were my last day on earth, would I think about the jobs I held, the books I read, the money I earned, or even the Napkin Notes I wrote? No. I would think only of the people I love, the relationships that have made my life full to bursting. The little girl who is somehow already a young woman.

Dear Emma, This week is going to be awesome. Don't forget to do your part. Love, Dad

CHAPTER 21

Dear Emma

Although each phase of Emma's life has had its own unique challenges, they were all relatively easy. As an infant, Emma didn't sleep through the night until she was eighteen months old. Most days I was thankful to be able to go into the office, knowing Lissa would have to trudge through the day without having fully recharged overnight. Really, I think that phase was the toughest for us so far. I'd say we've been incredibly blessed. We have had some very minor issues, but nothing that you wouldn't expect while raising a child.

And then Emma became a teenager. We waited for the storm

to hit. We braced ourselves. We're still waiting. I often think back to the nights when I rocked her to sleep and wished she could stay little. Even with all of the preparation, I want my little girl to always be my little girl. I certainly am not ready to have her go off to college!

Even though I want her to remain my little girl, I know it's my job to prepare her to become an adult. I don't just want her to be an average young woman. I want her to be extraordinary, well-rounded, graceful, humble, and remarkable. I want her to be able to tell her own story and have others enjoy listening.

Recently, we have purposely allowed Emma to start making some of her own decisions. It's appropriate. She is, after all, fourteen. For goodness sake, she'll be able to drive in just a year. She should be able to make some choices about her life! My dad wasn't very good about helping me with my decisions. He often said, "I made enough of my own mistakes. I won't be responsible for yours, too." Although I liked being able to make my own decisions, there were times I really needed my dad to override me and point me in a different direction. I have done my best to allow Emma to make her own decisions and guide her when I felt she needed it.

There are times that she has to make decisions on her own. We aren't always nearby. We trust that she will do her best.

Just a few weeks ago, we had our first "teenaged" run-in. She was on her own and made a bad choice. She clearly didn't ask herself, "What would Dad want me to choose?" I was greatly disappointed. I actually questioned my role as a father and wondered where I might have gone wrong. I know that teenagers get caught up in their own worlds and don't necessarily think of others, but this was hard for me to accept. I was genuinely hurt and wasn't sure what to do.

Emma walked on eggshells around me. She knew I was disappointed. She avoided looking me in the eye and really didn't want to talk with me. I think she thought I was angry. I was desperate for guidance on how to parent in this situation. Neither of us knew how to act around each other.

My dad isn't around to give me advice. I needed fatherly advice. I was giving this situation serious thought and everything fell into place. I don't know why I was struggling with this. I shouldn't have been thinking about it. I should have been praying. I thought of the only "father" I had left. What if I had disappointed God? How would he behave and how would he want me to behave?

God has always been there for me. He has never turned away,

nor will He. I will never turn away from Emma. How could I best communicate this to her? I remember a time when I was around seven years old. I got it in my head that life in my family was incredibly unfair and I "ran away." I was gone for a very short time. I received a book after that experience, *The Prodigal Son*. It was about a son who asked for his inheritance early, ran away, wasted the money, and sulked back to his father's home, in shame. He was planning on humbling himself and asking to become a servant. His father saw him returning, ran out to greet him, and immediately welcomed him back and prepared a feast in his son's honor. His brother questioned his father about this, and the father simply replied, "Son, you are always with me, and all that is mine is yours. It was fitting to celebrate and be glad, for your brother was dead, and is alive; he was lost, and is found" (Luke 31-32, ESV).

How many times in my life have I turned away from God? Did he ever turn away from me? No. He was always waiting for me to return, and was filled with joy when I did so.

I printed out a copy of these Bible verses and asked Emma to read them. After she had a chance to absorb the material, I sat with her and explained what the entire story meant. There are many nuances to understanding the words, the language, and the phrases. I shared with her my interpretation. The father was God, and the son, we humans. God is always there to support us, no matter how much we've messed up. We just have to turn around, go home, and ask.

Yes, she had made a mistake. She would probably make more. Yes, her actions might, from time to time, disappoint me.

I looked her in the eye. I will *always* love you. I will *always* be there for you. I will *always* support you.

I will *always* come get you.

It was an appropriate conversation. I think she understood my views on being her father. I didn't start out meaning to talk to her about this. I really wanted to talk to her about choices and behavior.

I think I ended up having more impact with the discussion as it was.

Life would be wonderfully easy if I could sit in the glider chair each night around 10 P.M., feed Emma her bottle, and rock her back to sleep.

I wouldn't change where I am for anything.

Dear Emma, Make your life story worth telling.
Love, Dad

CHAPTER 22

My Life List

Appearing throughout this book are little life lessons. They are addressed to Emma. That's because instead of writing a chapter on my bucket list, or all the things I want to do before I die, I've been creating a Life List for Emma. A list of all the things I want to make sure she experiences in life. The stuff I want her to learn along the way. Some of them are big; some of them are small. But these are the things I want her to know.

Obviously, I wish I wasn't sharing it in this way. I wish I knew for sure that I was going to be there, always. To walk with her through life. To talk to her about what college she should go to. To advise her on whatever relationships she might develop over the years. To help her write her college admissions essays. To quiz her for her first job interview.

But we all know that may not be possible.

I hate that we're there. But we all must acknowledge that possibility.

Napkin Notes isn't about dying. Napkin Notes is about living. It's about communicating important lessons to our kids. It's about sharing every day how much we care. It's about realizing the power we have every day to make a difference. You may not think that a few words on a piece of paper matter. They do. I hope this book shows that.

Stop wasting time. Stop making excuses. Who is most important to you? Do you tell them you love them every day? What are you teaching your kids? What values are you imparting to them? Can you take the time to write a note? To have a conversation? To put away the phone, turn off the TV, and find a way to connect? Every day?

The thing is Napkin Notes is simple. I'm not a remarkable guy. I've just somehow been given a platform to remind us of how very straightforward this is. It's about love. It's about communication.

It's about making small efforts that have great meaning.

Will you join me? Will you become a Napkin Notes dad or a Napkin Notes mom or a Napkin Notes wife or husband?

This is what matters. Nothing else.

Emma's Life List

1. Learn how to take criticism with grace.

2. Learn to give a toast.

3. Have a boss you love.

4. Get fired.

5. Become a lifelong learner.

6. Don't be afraid to quit.

7. Love someone when you know it won't work out.

8. Give away money.

9. Your significant other should not be your reason for life.

10. Receive gifts gracefully.

11. Learn basic car functions.

12. Your hairstyle isn't you.

13. Be willing to learn from your elders.

14. Give meaningful gifts.

15. Always do your best.

16. Don't speed.

17. Don't drink and drive. Ever.

18. Be comfortable using public transportation.

19. Get lost in a country where you don't know the language.

20. You alone are responsible for your happiness.

21. Don't compare your successes or failures to others' successes or failures.

22. Don't be late to class.

23. Read the recommended reading.

24. Work a part-time job to pay for college.

25. Make unlikely friends.

26. Don't be greedy.

27. Work as a waitress.

28. Befriend a restaurant owner.

29. Learn to make a signature cocktail.

30. Don't eat ice cream unless it's your favorite flavor.

31. Don't do drugs.

32. Accept your feelings.

33. Control your behavior. You can't control your feelings, but don't let them lead you to poor choices.

34. Put your phone down.

35. Things are things.

36. Look people in the eye. Use a firm handshake. Hug when it's appropriate.

37. Keep six months of expenses saved.

38. Don't sleep around.

39. Lose gracefully and then learn. Win even more gracefully.

40. Life is too short to work for a jerk.

41. If you can't talk about it, you shouldn't do it.

42. Learn to play an instrument well.

43. Become comfortable with the digital world.

44. Learn to forgive.

45. Don't give up.

46. Stand up for people.

47. Exercise some each week. This isn't an option.

48. Learn to say no.

49. Learn to say yes.

50. Learn to be quiet.

51. Call when you're going to be late.

52. Use condoms.

53. Always be positive.

54. Learn how to say "I was wrong."

55. Don't hate yourself in the morning.

56. Give your friend your last dollar.

57. You are a leader. Lead.

58. Build a team better than you.

59. It's okay to have a job that's a little bit lower than your skills.

EPILOGUE

I'm the only person stirring in the house this early in the morning. It's dark still, and there is a chill on the kitchen floor as I walk to fetch my first cup of coffee. The warmth from the mug eases the morning routine. I open the refrigerator to gather the food for lunch. There is fresh fruit from the crisper and some homemade strawberry jam in a jar. The fruit is washed and cut, and the jam is spread on bread with peanut butter. Fresh water is a must. Lunch wouldn't be complete without a little treat. "Should I toss in a cookie?" I think aloud. I decide that a small cookie won't harm anyone. Lunch is always made and packed with love. Many people would consider this lunch complete, but not me.

The moment of truth comes. I have always experienced a two-second fear of an empty napkin. I grab a pen—the same pen I've used for years to write countless Napkin Notes for my daughter, Emma—and I sip some coffee as I contemplate the emptiness of white napkins. I pause. Is there something special going on today at school? I don't know of anything. I pour a second cup of coffee and begin to write . . .

"Don't forget to be AWESOME! You are one of the most incredible kids I know and I am so proud of you."

That is a good message for the day. I smile and hope this message has a great impact.

I pull out a second napkin and write "Do more of what makes you awesome! I love you!" I love using the word "awesome" as often as I can on Napkin Notes.

I hear feet bounding down the stairs as I finish folding the napkins.

"Whatcha doing, Grandpa?"

"Oh, just finishing up your lunch. I made one for your brother too. I am really glad to be here for your first day of school this year. Are you excited?"

"Yeah, I think middle school will be a lot of fun. I am ready for the big leagues now!" she jokes.

I hand each of my grandchildren a lunch and give them a kiss good-bye.

Emma smiles at me and says, "I'll be back in a few minutes, Dad." She kisses me on the cheek and drives her kids to school.

EMMA'S TOP FIVE NAPKIN NOTES

I've received so many Napkin Notes over the years that it's hard to pick my favorites. But below are some that stick out to me. Typically, I tend to like Napkin Notes that have quotes that make you think. The quote often seems simple at first, but there's something deeper going on when you stop and think about it.

Although we never expected my dad would write a book about Napkin Notes, I'm glad that there is something out there in the world that my dad and I have done together. It will hardly be my final mark, but it is definitely something special.

More than anything I want to say thank you to my dad. Even though he's the one right now who shouldn't have to be strong, he is the one being strong throughout this situation. I'm so proud of him.

Dear Emma, You can't win if you don't play.
Love, Dad

I received this Napkin Note shortly after I was chosen to be on the Rockville All-Star softball team. The message in this quote never fails to motivate me to go to softball practice or to try my hardest for something. It helps me realize that I need to remember the feeling that I achieve after winning a game or having a good practice. I can't have that feeling unless I play. I have to take the initiative to make things happen.

Dear Emma, Remember that girl
who looked down from the jungle gym as
Colin was saying, "I'll save you, Emma!"
and you replied, "I'll save myself!"?
Be that girl. Be brave.
Love, Dad

My dad has always encouraged me to be strong, independent, and confident. This note brings back old memories and it reminds me that I don't need anyone else to "save me." It reinforces my self-confidence and reminds me that I can be an independent girl who solves her own problems and makes smart decisions . . . the kind of girl that my dad is raising me to be.

Dear Emma, Sometimes when I need a miracle, I look into your eyes and see that I've already created one.
Love, Dad

I adore this note not only because it boosts my confidence, but because it reminds me that I am able to make my father feel better. It shows me that I am able to make a difference in my dad's outlook on his life and his health. This is important to me because I know that if he is feeling well physically it will mean more time for us to spend together. I struggle when I know he feels sick from the medicine he takes. It can really knock him down and I don't like to see him suffer.

Dear Emma, It's been a crazy week
for us. Let's not forget to have an
awesome weekend together!!
Love, Dad

This note brings back good memories. I received it after one of the trips my parents and I took to New York. These trips were fun; however, they were rather stressful for us because we got practically no sleep and were on a tight schedule in order to be on television shows. We were all relieved to be at home, and when I received this note during lunch it made me hopeful for the following weekend, when things might return to normal. It made me smile to realize my dad knew that I was tired, and it helped me get through the tough school day.

Life doesn't have to be perfect
to be wonderful.
—Annette Funicello

This note isn't as inspirational to me as the others, though it still means a lot to me. It doesn't have a quote that relates directly to me, and it isn't a story from my childhood. What makes this note special to me is that it brings me hope for my dad. His life certainly isn't perfect. But that doesn't mean that he can't make the most of it and work through the cancer to make his life wonderful.

The Note Writer's Philosophy

- *If you pack a lunch for someone, include a note! Everyone enjoys a note with their lunch.*

- *If your child is eating, give them a napkin. Using a napkin is a sign of good table manners.*

- *Deep thoughts are not required for a Napkin Note. Sometimes it's better to communicate a simple thought or idea.*

- *Writing a Napkin Note tells the recipient you were thinking of them. And when they read it, they'll be thinking of you. It's a good cycle.*

- *Make your child's lunch for them. Don't use too many prepackaged goods. Wash, mix, cut, and wrap it yourself. You'll be connected to the food. You'll be connected to what your child eats.*

- *Buying lunch is the last choice. It is much more difficult to include a note if your child buys lunch at school. Your homemade lunch will also taste better and be a healthier choice.*

- *Write notes to children who cannot yet read. It's never too early to start. Draw stars and hearts. You can use basic words that communicate your family values like "love" and "happy."*

- *You're never too busy to write a note. It takes less than five seconds to write out "I love you!"*

How to Write a Napkin Note

Staring at a blank napkin can be tough. I understand. It's early in the morning and you might not have had your daily recommended allowance of caffeine yet.

It's important to recognize the meaning behind why you are motivated to write a note. What do you want the reader to receive? What do they need to receive?

The first step for me is to say a quick prayer. If you don't pray, that's okay; just take a moment and think about how this napkin might transform into something more than a simple note.

I write two basic types of Napkin Notes, and what you use will be personal.

The first type is a motivational quote. I find these everywhere.

I am an avid reader and pay attention to things that would make a good Napkin Note for Emma. The quote should be meaningful to the day. Don't forget to credit the author. There are plenty of examples throughout the book, on our website, and on our social media pages.

If your child is reluctant at first to receive a note from Mom or Dad and doesn't want to be embarrassed, try writing a code.

- *Hide a note at the bottom of a paper lunch bag.*

- *Use acronyms, such as MTFBWY (May the Force be with you) or DFTBA (Don't forget to be awesome).*

- *Write small notes on the inside of napkins. A varsity move is when you write something like "It's what's on the inside that matters" and then on the inside of the napkin "You're awesome!"*

The second type of Napkin Note is the most important one for me. It's highly personal. This is the one that really rocks and takes both effort and heart. Here's how I start:

"Dear Emma, I am so proud . . ."

And then I write what I'm proud of. You can't just say that

you're proud. You have to say why and give a clear, concrete example.

Here's how I might finish this type of Napkin Note:

"Dear Emma, I am so proud of how you play softball. You are an enthusiastic player and a great sport. I love to watch you play. Love, Dad."

Fold the Napkin Note in half, with the writing on the inside, and place it gently in the lunch bag.

Smile. Know that you've done your part to connect with someone today.

MORE THAN NAPKIN NOTES

I am thankful that I have a daily opportunity to write a Napkin Note to Emma. I made the decision long ago that a homemade lunch was the best choice for her. I am convinced that even when I add a less-than-healthy item, such as a mini candy or a cookie, Emma's lunch has fewer fat calories and more whole foods than she would ever receive in a school-purchased lunch. It's hard. Don't get me wrong. Looking into the pantry and refrigerator each morning and deciding what to pack is as difficult as staring at a blank napkin and composing a note. Both packing the lunch and writing the Napkin Note take effort, sometimes all the energy I have that early in the morning.

It's worth it.

We continue to move into a more digital world. We love our smartphones and apps. Handwritten notes are taking on a greater meaning than they have had in quite some time. A handwritten note is tangible. A handwritten note can be saved. It takes time and effort to both write and read. A handwritten note implicitly carries a deep meaning. The author takes the time to compose and write. The recipient takes the time to read and absorb the meaning of the note. It's a good cycle.

Napkin Notes don't have to be on napkins. Napkin Notes aren't just for children. Let's expand the definition of Napkin Notes to include any short note delivered to a loved one and see what the possibilities would include. At the very least, this allows us to forgo the need to pack a homemade lunch.

Sticky Notes on a Bathroom Mirror

This is a great option if you leave the house before your loved one. It's extra fun if you use a dry-erase marker, but you can't save a "note" written like that.

Hidden Notes

I have a dear friend, Adam Mead, who peppered his house with notes before a business trip. He hid notes in pockets, in an oven mitt, and in places you'd probably never think to hide a note. His family was finding notes for the entire duration of his business trip.

Darth Vader Heads

Another dear friend presented me with plastic Darth Vader heads. Inside each one was a small candy and a quote, like a personalized Star Wars fortune cookie. I opened one on days when I needed some additional motivation or support.

Notes Inside Books

We are avid readers, and there are books always lying around the house. When you really want to leave a note in the future, pop one well after the bookmark. It will remain there, waiting for the reader to turn the page. This works equally as well for schoolbooks!

Paper Plate Notes

This is a great option for homeschool lunchtime or picnics. There is a lot of area around the circumference of a paper plate for long messages.

Picture Notes

What do you do if you want to send a lunch Napkin Note but the child can't yet read? Send a picture! Print off a series of pictures of family favorites: a pet, the home, stuffed animals, a birthday cake, or family members! This will help develop an anticipation for opening the lunch and finding something special. As children learn basic reading skills, you can start to write simple words on a napkin and draw a picture associated with that word.

Notes on the Front Seat

I received my first note from Lissa on December 2, 2013. It was my first day on a new job and she had placed a note on the front seat of my truck. I still have it in there to this day. You can also tuck a note behind the sun visor if you don't care if it's read right away!

Mailed Notes

There's no reason to forget the most traditional way of sending a note: the mail. Everyone enjoys receiving something other than a bill or junk mail. You can even send a series of notes to be received each day of the week.

Wallet or Purse Notes

Take a small slip of paper with heartfelt words, fold it in half, and tuck it next to a debit card or driver's license.

Notes Inside a Laptop

Write a note and place it inside the laptop covering the trackpad. Close the lid and let the owner be surprised later!

Kitchen Bulletin Board Notes

This is a great way to leave notes for various family members and initiate a back and forth communication. Lissa will often write dinner plans for the week on our board, and I will occasionally write a sad face next to the item that I don't want! Families with younger children can use this to choose a word for the week. This word can be important to the family and should be discussed together. Important family words should be short for those learning to read: "joy," "love," "happy," "family," "home," "true," "give," "share," and "trust" are great words to start!

Notes on the Bottom of a Mouse

What a great way to turn a trick into a message of love! Use a sticky note. Write a message and then apply the note to the bottom of the computer mouse. Nothing will happen when the user tries to move the mouse. The recipient will find the note when they investigate.

All of these examples are great for family and friends. Writing a personalized note will strengthen the relationship. Repeating the action can carry that relationship to a new level of communication.

It's worth it.

I'd like to suggest another area where we could significantly improve positive communication. Workplace communication is completely dependent on e-mail. The average employee sends or receives over 105 e-mails per day. Even if a manager were to send a "Nice job" e-mail, there is a high likelihood it would be lost in the sea of daily e-mails.

Imagine the impact if your manager handwrote a note about what a great job you did on a project and left it on your desk! How would you feel? How would the manager feel after writing this note?

GRATITUDE

I can't begin to express thanks for everyone who has helped shape my life and prepare for this battle.

Thank you to:

My wife, Lissa, for being my rock. You have loved me when I have been unlovable. You carry my weight when I cannot. Here's to beating the odds!

My mom, who has acted with selflessness and kindness to help me in my battles.

My sister, Colleen, I am sorry about the paint. I won't tell mom if you don't. Give those kids a kiss for me. I'm eternally grateful you are my sister.

My dad, for making me earn every "win" I ever had. I sure miss you and wish you were here.

My Aunt Ruth, for reminding me of the things that really matter.

My cousin, Jo-Anne Estes Ebensteiner, for coming to my rescue and walking with me along this journey more than once.

All of the Callaghans and Keoughs. I am eternally grateful to be part of both family lines.

My friends in Port Leyden, for providing such a great place to grow up and also for your support in April.

My first real boss, Ed Flisak, who taught me the value of knowing what my job was and learning to do that well.

Father Dan Brady, who asked me the hard questions and already knew the answers.

Terry Martin and the Knights of Columbus for saving me. I was desperately in need of spiritual guidance when you appeared.

Dr. Tim Bradford, for believing in fighting the good fight, and for your dedication to my best medical program.

Dr. Craig Swainey, for bringing God into the exam room and for the steadfast belief that I'll beat this.

René Haines, for your continued friendship, support, and guidance.

Adam Mead, for your spiritual insight and being a darned good friend.

Kris Hall, for your friendship and getting me home when I most needed it.

Ted McCall, for showing me how to be a best friend for thirty-five years.

Jim Murray, for your unending enthusiasm for my crazy ideas.

My mentors at Circuit City: Theresa Klotz, Dawn von Bechmann, Kay Thornberry, and Jennifer Jones.

Kim Zirkle, who took a chance on me when she had no business doing so.

Alex Sheen, for enabling me to express an implied promise and fulfill a very difficult one.

Cait Hoyt, for believing in our story and mission, and making it your own.

Lisa Sharkey, for expediting my visit with Memorial Sloan Kettering and helping us to share our story.

Amy Bendell, for valuable guidance during our storytelling process.

Cindy DiTiberio, for your patience, guidance, support, and

enthusiasm, without which this book would not exist.

Everyone who has prayed for me and supported this journey.

And last, but certainly not least, Nicole Kiniry. Nicole, you have been one of my biggest supporters. You make me look forward to visiting my doctors. You always have a reassuring word and a steady voice. You watch out for me as if I were your brother, and I couldn't walk this path without you to help me navigate. You have always been my guardian angel. Thank you for being there for me. I'd never make it to my appointments without you, and thank you for always giving me vanilla contrast. I swear, I'll invent Guinness-flavored contrast soon.

KEEP WRITING

Facebook facebook.com/napkinnotes

Twitter @napkinnotesdad

Tumblr napkinnotesdad.tumblr.com

Pinterest pinterest.com/napkinnotesdad

Instagram napkinnotesdad

Website www.napkinnotesdad.com

E-mail garth@napkinnotesdad.com

Phone 804-480-4127